WE DARE TO DREAM

WE DARE TO DREAM

DOING THEOLOGY AS ASIAN WOMEN

Edited by
Virginia Fabella M.M.
and
Sun Ai Lee Park

ORBIS BOOKS

Maryknoll, New York 10545

The Catholic Foreign Mission Society of America (Maryknoll) recruits and trains people for overseas missionary service. Through Orbis Books, Maryknoll aims to foster the international dialogue that is essential to mission. The books published, however, reflect the opinions of their authors and are not meant to represent the official position of the society.

First published by the Asian Women's Resource Centre for Culture and Theology and the Asian Office of the Women's Commission of the Ecumenical Association of Third World Theologians (EATWOT), P.O.B. 314, Greenhills, Metro Manila 1502, Philippines, copyright © 1989 by AWCCT, Hong Kong

U.S. edition published 1990 by Orbis Books, Maryknoll, NY 10545
Printed in the United States of America

ISBN 0-88344-673-1

Contents

Introduction   vii

PART ONE
REWORKING THEOLOGICAL THEMES

1. Christology from an Asian Woman's Perspective   3
   Virginia Fabella (Philippines)

2. Christology and Women   15
   Monica Melanchton (India)

3. Ecclesiology and Women: A View from Taiwan   24
   Lily Kuo Wang (Taiwan)

4. New Ways of Being Church   33
   I. A Catholic Perspective   33
   Christine Tse (Hong Kong)
   II. A Protestant Perspective   44
   Yong Ting Jin (Malaysia)

5. Woman and the Holy Spirit: From an Indian Perspective   52
   Crescy John (India)

PART TWO
REFLECTING ON ASIAN REALITIES

6. Peace, Unification and Women   65
   I. A Bible Study   65
   Lee Oo Chung (Korea)
   II. A Theological Reflection   72
   Sun Ai Lee Park (Korea)

7. Biblical Concept of Human Sexuality: Challenge to Tourism   83
   Elizabeth Dominguez (Philippines)

8. The Emergence of Asian Feminist Consciousness of Culture   92
   and Theology
      Kwok Pui-lan (Hong Kong)

9. Redefining Religious Commitment in the Philippine Context   101
      Mary John Mananzan (Philippines)

PART THREE
DOING THEOLOGY AS ASIAN WOMEN

10. Towards an Indian Feminist Theology   117
       Aruna Gnanadason (India)

11. Feminist Theology in the Korean Church   127
       Ahn Sang Nim (Korea)

12. "Han-pu-ri" Doing Theology from Korean Women's Perspective   135
       Chung Hyun Kyung (Korea)

13. Final Statement: Asian Church Women Speak   147
       *(Asian Women's consultation, Manila, Philippines,
       November 21-30, 1985)*

14. Conference Statement: Consultation on Asian Women's Theology 151
       (Singapore, November 20-29, 1987)

Contributors   155

Introduction

Doing theology from the perspective of Asian women is a relatively new phenomenon. Since the 1970s, women theologians in Asia have felt the need of a theology that is more cognizant of their context and inclusive of the women's viewpoint. However, with very few exceptions, their efforts in general were more reflective of the thinking of Third World male liberation theologians or First World feminists. More recently, Christian women have become aware that without their distinctive voices as Asians and as women, the emerging theologies in Asia cannot be liberating or relevant, not for themselves or for the Church or society at large.

I

The collection of essays in this volume reflects efforts of Christian women in Asia to do theology from their own particular perspective. These women are part of two Asian women's networks whose goal is to promote a liberating and transforming theology from the perspective of Asian women: The Women's Commission of the Ecumenical Association of Third World Theologians (EATWOT) and the Asian Women's Resource Centre for Culture and Theology. As Asians, these women take their history and context seriously, and examine both their past and present. As women, together they take a critical look at their own and other women's experience, trace the roots of their secondary and subservient position in Church and society, and venture towards a new world of just and reciprocal relationships.

The EATWOT Women's Commission was formed only in 1983. Realizing that even in an association of liberation theologians the women's contribution was not fully appreciated or understood by the members, the women created the Commission, formulated a five-year plan of action, and established some general guidelines for their work. Using the basic methodology of the Association that begins with the experience of poor and oppressed peoples and includes a serious examination of their socio-economic, political, and religio-cultural reality, the EATWOT women sought to rework some of the main theological themes from Third World women's perspective. This they did in a collaborative way, first on a national, then on a continent-wide, and finally on an intercontinental level. Four of the articles in this collection are from the Asian Women's Consultation held in Manila, Philippines in 1985, and from the Intercontinental Women's Conference held in Oaxtepec, Mexico in 1986, three of which were originally published in the Orbis book, *With*

Passion and Compassion: Third World Women Doing Theology.[1] Five other essays are by women who are associated with the EATWOT Women's Commission, some of which have initially been published in theological or ecumenical reviews.[2]

The Asian Women's Resource Centre was established in 1988, with its base in Hong Kong. Besides collecting resource material on culture and theology as these relate to women, the Centre tries to support and strengthen Asian women's efforts to do theology in their own context. Several of the essays included in this present collection are by women who belong to the Centre's network.

One of the Centre's major activities is to organize and coordinate women's theological programs and consultations. The Asian Women Theologians' Conference which took place in Singapore in 1987 and was patterned after the Manila Consultation brought thirty-two women from sixteen countries together. Two articles and the final document are the contribution of the Singapore consultation to this volume.

Perhaps the most widely known project of the Women's Resource Centre is the publication of *In God's Image.*[3] Initiated by Sun Ai Lee Park in 1982 and first published in Singapore with the help of friends from the Christian Conference of Asia (CCA), the journal is "an Asian Christian women's effort to provide a forum for expressing our reality, our struggles, our faith reflections and our aspirations for change."[4] When CCA was forced to move out of Singapore, it was decided to transfer the publishing of *In God's Image* to Hong Kong and place it under the auspices of the Resource Centre. The 2,000 copies of each issue of the journal are circulated not only in Asia, but also in Africa, Latin America, North America and Europe. *In God's Image* is the source of the remainder of our essays.

II

The essays are divided into three main groupings. The first grouping, entitled "Reworking Theological Themes," consists of essays showing efforts to indicate some of the shortcomings of the male-oriented formulations of the past, and to approach the traditional themes of christology, ecclesiology and pneumatology in a fresh way, from an Asian woman's viewpoint. This is an inclusive view which takes women's, and not only men's, humanity and experience seriously, and discerns both the life-enhancing and death-endorsing aspects of our faith tradition and theology, especially as these have affected the marginalized—who are mostly women.

The second group of essays, under the title "Reflecting on Asian Realities," shows how our Asian reality affects women and, more often than not, perpetuates their exploitation, multiplies their oppression, and intensifies their suffering as women. Unfortunately, Christianity, as well as other religious traditions in Asia, with their patriarchal structures, attitudes and practices, have contributed to women's pain and discrimination in similar ways. The

authors' concern about the subordinate role and use of women in Asian society is matched by the challenge they pose. Not only women's reality, but our world *can* change if we are willing to undertake the tasks to be done, and with the collaboration of Asian men, to work towards the elimination of whatever dehumanizes both men and women alike.

The third set of essays, entitled "Doing Theology as Asian Women," demonstrates how much has been done by women within a relatively short period of time. But it also indicates how much more there is to be done if Christian theology is to be truly relevant to the Asian context, which is marked by poverty and dominated by patriarchal institutions on the one hand, and characterized by a diversity of religions and cultures on the other.

There were problems in selecting essays for this volume. We had three criteria: first, the work must be contextualized, that is, it starts with an aspect of our Asian experience and is rooted in our Asian reality. It necessarily includes a critical examination of the context, not a mere description. Second, it must be theological, with references to our faith tradition, and not simply be a historical, sociological or analytical study of the Asian context and peoples. And third, it must be from the perspective of women that shows an awareness of the subordinate and oftentimes degrading situation of women and reveals a commitment to work towards its transformation. Only a handful of the essays we reviewed met the three criteria.

On the other hand, other articles could have been included in this volume, but there were difficulties with deadlines. This is also the reason why there are gaps in the contributions. Some well-known Asian women theologians are noticeably absent; some countries boasting of associations of women in theology are not represented in this book. For sources, both editors of this collection relied on the EATWOT Women's Commission and the Asian Resource Centre, to which both of us belong. However, our hope is to have a second volume that would include a wider range of writers and a broader scope of topics that are reflective of the Asian women's reality.

III

We wish to conclude our Introduction with a word of thanks to all the women who have contributed to this volume, both directly and indirectly, and to all the others, who have worked behind the scene or have lent their generous support to make the production of this book possible.

We hope that the publishing of this collection of essays will encourage other Asian women to put their reflections in writing and to engage in the production of serious theological resources from the perspective of women.

Unless our thoughts as women are known and our voices heard, the work towards rearticulating Christian theology in Asia will remain truncated. God's face will only be half seen and God's voice only half heard. If the emerging Asian theology is to be significant to men and women alike, our contribution as Asian women cannot be isolated or simply attached as a token appendage, but must form an integral part of the whole.

We hope that Christian women in Asia will take this pressing task to heart. By sharing our experiences and reflections, we can also further our solidarity not only among women in Asia but with all women who strive from "bondage to bonding." It is in working together that we can begin changing the face of the earth. Our vision is to see men and women in communities of genuine partnership, with true reciprocity and mutual respect, in communities that care not only for people but for our whole planet earth. We envision a new world; a transformed world; a world that truly mirrors God's design; a just, caring, and peace-filled world—indeed, a new creation. We dare to dream...

Virginia Fabella and Sun Ai Lee Park

NOTES

1. Virginia Fabella and Mercy Amba Oduyoye, eds., *With Passion and Compassion: Third World Women Doing Theology* (Maryknoll, New York: Orbis Books, 1988).

2. Chung Hyun Kyung's article, " 'Han-pu-ri': Doing Theology from Korean Women's Perspective,"is reprinted from the *Ecumenical Review,* Vol. 40, No.1, January 1988. The *Ecumenical Review* is a quarterly journal published by the WCC, 150 Route de Ferney, Ch-1211 Geneva 20, Switzerland.

Mary John Mananzan's essay will appear in a forthcoming Orbis Book publication, Marc H. Ellis and Otto Maduro eds., *The Future of Liberation Theology: Essays in Honour of Gustavo Gutierrez* (Maryknoll, New York, 1989).

3. *In God's Image* is a quarterly journal published by the Asian Women's Resource Centre, 566 Nathan Road, Kiu Kin Mansion 6/F, Kowloon, Hong Kong.

4. *In God's Image*, cover, September 1987.

Part One

REWORKING THEOLOGICAL THEMES

1

Christology from an Asian Woman's Perspective

Virginia Fabella (Philippines)

Asian women are beginning to articulate their own christologies. For too long, what we are to believe about Jesus Christ and what he is to mean for us have been imposed on us by our colonizers, by the Western world, by a patriarchal church, and by male scholars and spiritual advisers. But now we are discovering Jesus Christ for ourselves. What we say may not be anything new; what is important is now we are saying it ourselves. To the question posed by Jesus "Who do people say that I am?" we are giving answers that reflect not only what we encounter in Scriptures, but also our reality and experience as Asian women. Thus our christologies are not only interpretations of Jesus, but confessions of our faith in this Jesus who has made a difference in our lives, and not only as a speculative activity, but as active engagement in striving towards the full humanity Jesus came to bring.

Although women doing theology and constructing christologies have experienced discrimination and "tokenism" in both church and society, ours is a life of privilege compared to that of other women in Asia. The reality, backed by cases and statistics, is that "in all spheres of Asian society, women are dominated, dehumanized and dewomanized...viewed as inferior beings who must always subordinate themselves to the so-called male supremacy...treated with bias and condescension. In Asia and all over the world, the myth of the subservient, servile Asian women is blatantly peddled to reinforce the dominant male stereotype image."[1] Thus, even if this is an attempt to express "my" christology, I need to take into account these countless women, whether they believe in Jesus Christ or not. Jesus' liberating and humanizing message has meaning for all women struggling for full humanity and their rightful place in history, for Jesus' message not only liberates but also empowers.

3

I

Christology is at the heart of all theology for it is Jesus who has revealed to us the deepest truths about God. In his humanity, Jesus revealed God as a loving God who cares for the weakest and lowliest and wills the full humanity and salvation of all, men and women alike. In his humanity, Jesus has shown us what it means to be truly human, to have life abundantly, to be saved. Thus christology is central and integral to any talk about God, human-God relationship and all right relationships and to any discussion about salvation and liberation.

There are important issues which any christology must deal with. However, here I will only touch on those that have a bearing on my being Asian and woman, those that are more pertinent to the Asian context and the issue of gender. Feminist theologians in the U.S. have raised the question of the maleness of Jesus. Among Asian women, the maleness of Jesus has not been a problem for we see it as "accidental" to the salvific process. His maleness was not essential but functional. By being male, Jesus could repudiate more effectively the male definition of humanity and show the way to a right and just male-female relationship, challenging both men and women to change their life patterns. Historically, however, christology has been patriarchalized and has been the doctrine of the Christian tradition most used against women.[2] Thus the feminists' question stands.

An issue facing christology pertinent to our Asian context is the new understandings of salvation in different cultures. Salvation/liberation takes on different meanings within a reality of massive poverty and multiple oppression on the one hand, and of religious, cultural and ideological plurality on the other. In a continent where 97 percent of the people are not Christian, can we claim Jesus Christ as the savior of the whole world? How is he the unique and universal savior when the majority in Asia alone have never heard of him or have even ignored him in their quest for a better world? Some of the Asian faiths offer salvation which relates more closely than Christianity to the soteriological depths of our cultures, to the desire for liberation from both individual and organized greed.[3] Have we listened to what other major faiths have had to say about Jesus, especially those who have seriously grappled with his mystery, or have we as Christians tended to be "protective" and exclusive about Jesus?

These and other pertinent issues need to be addressed in the process of constructing an Asian christology, a process which is just beginning. Theologians like Aloysius Pieris have indicated guidelines for this effort,[4] but these have not included anything that speaks directly to women's reality. Though the christology be educed from the depths of our cultures and expressed in Asia's soteriological idiom, the result will not be relevant unless it takes into account the women's experience, perspective and contribution. Only then can we agree with Indian theologian George Soares that spelling

4

out the place of Jesus in Asia is "Asia's ultimate challenge to Christian theology."[5]

<h1 style="text-align:center">II</h1>

In formulating my christology, I shall reflect on some of the important christological themes and consequent implications. Every christology focuses on the life and significance of Jesus Christ; therefore, the historical Jesus plays a central role. It is necessary to return to the Jesus of history, to the man Jesus who was born and who lived on our continent, whose life was rooted in Jewish culture and religious tradition. By his life, words, and actions, Jesus of Nazareth has shown us the meaning of humanity and divinity. To bypass history is to make an abstraction of Jesus and thus to distort his person, mission and message of love and salvation. Moreover, it is only in reference to the historical Jesus that we can test the authenticity of our Jesus images and see how closely they relate to the reality.

Jesus' core message centered on the kingdom of God: The reign of God is near; repent and believe in the good news (Mk 1:15). His central message focused not on himself but on God and our response to God's gift of the kingdom. Seeing God's reign as imminent and becoming conscious of a special call, Jesus proclaimed its coming and urged the people to reform their lives, believe the good news, and be saved. To enter the kingdom meant to change one's ways of behaving and relating. The notion of God's kingdom was a familiar one to the people for it is contained in Hebrew Scriptures and intertestamental literature, although by Jesus' time it had acquired a variety of interpretations. For this reason, Jesus aligned himself with John the Baptist and accepted John's baptism, for John preached the same message to the "crowds," the ordinary men and women, demanding repentance. This was so unlike the stance of the other groups: the Essenes, with their passive, elitist interpretation of the Kingdom, or the legalistic Pharisees or aristocratic Sadducees.

As an itinerant preacher/healer, Jesus drew a following for he performed signs and spoke with authority, and what he taught he practiced. He chose twelve apostles whom he instructed in the way of the kingdom. Although his message was for all, the people he attracted most were those on the fringes of society, those who were in "most need of salvation." However, not everything Jesus taught and practiced in terms of the kingdom was familiar or easy to understand, accept or follow. His message included what others have never taught: the inclusive character of God's reign. Jesus lived out his teaching by freely associating with, and showing preference for, the poor and marginalized—sinners, outcasts, women. They were the last who had become first; the humble who had become exalted.

Jesus' attitude towards women and treatment of them was most uncommon even for a "good" Jew of his day, for he was not only considerate of them and treated them with deep respect, but even acted contrary to the prevailing customs and practices. Women were among the non-persons in society, mere chattel. But Jesus never ignored them when they approached him for healing; they were human beings worth making whole again. They were entitled to the "life in abundance;" they were worthy of learning the Torah. He not only valued them as friends but affirmed their trustworthiness and capability to be disciples, witnesses, missionaries, and apostles.[6]

Jesus taught something else that was new and more difficult still: that love of God and neighbor must include love of enemies. From the time of Ezra, Jews and Samaritans had become irrevocable enemies. Yet by parable and example, Jesus made his point to "love your enemies; do good to those who hate you" (Lk 6:27). The good Samaritan's concern for his neighbor made a model to follow; the Samaritan woman who gives him to drink becomes his missionary to her people. Jesus likewise showed compassion on the foreigner, being touched by a Roman centurion's "faith" and concern for his servant, and allowing himself to be challenged by the entreaties and confidence of a Syrophoenician woman. Thus Jesus showed that to live a truly human life, one lives a life-in-relation, demonstrated by care and service even to the least: the women, the enemy, the outsider. But this was not all. Jesus spelled out what right human relationship is in practice, what it means to "love one another": there is no lording it over others; even masters shall serve; right relation to one's neighbor has priority over temple worship; discipleship is above blood relationship; only by losing one's life shall one find it. What a liberating message for the women; they were the dominated, the taken-for-granted, the one-sided servers, the "mother of" or "daughter of." Jesus made clear what being human means; only thus can one enter the kingdom of God. And the invitation is open to all.

Jesus' words and deeds brought him into conflict not only with the Jewish religious authorities but also with the Roman leadership. Even as he announced the kingdom, he denounced hypocrisy, oppression and misuse of power. The Romans were threatened by the former, the religious leaders by the latter. Seeing that his end was near, Jesus "bequeathed" to his apostles the basic meaning of his message and ministry at a last meal together. That very night, Jesus was arrested, tried in two courts, found guilty of sedition by the Romans and sentenced to death by crucifixion. Jesus did not resist; he understood the consequences of his word and works in fidelity to God's call.

III

For the apostles, Jesus' death was a shame and a scandal which shook their faith and shattered their hopes. In fact, afraid of Roman reprisals, they dispersed, and only a few disciples, mostly women, remained with Jesus as he died on the cross, to all semblances a failure. But then, the unexpected happened. The disciples, beginning with the women, started to report appearances which they gradually began to identify with Jesus as they experienced peace and forgiveness. He had "risen from the dead!" The apostles reassembled and recalled all that Jesus taught and did, and recognized God's confirmation of his words and deeds in raising him from the dead. Their new experience of Jesus radically transformed them into people of courage and faith, impelling them to continue Jesus' ministry and spread his message of salvation as they witnessed to him as their Lord and God. The small Jesus movement/community began to grow and extend to the four corners of the earth. All this "unexpected" is the reality of the resurrection. By his rising, Jesus has conquered death, the "first fruits of those who sleep" (1 Cor 15:20), embodying the advent of God's promise of salvation, signaling the dawning of God's kingdom. By his rising, Jesus is confirmed as the Christ and God's true son, the model of redeemed humanity, the incarnation of true divinity, no longer limited to the particularities of his maleness and Jewishness. Jesus Christ lives and continues to affect, renew, and give hope to the millions all over the globe who would believe and follow him. Jesus Christ is alive and we encounter him in our sisters and brothers.

The apostles' resurrection faith enabled them not only to understand God as Jesus revealed God in his life, death and rising, but also to interpret Jesus' death differently. The apostles and other disciples had taken Jesus' death as a disappointing, shameful end of an eschatological prophet whose life failed to bring about the kingdom he preached. Their Easter faith, however, told them that Jesus' death was not a failure but a fulfillment. This later gave rise to varied explanations, but the one that perdured defined Jesus' death as an offering to God as sacrifice and reconciliation. Jesus is the suffering servant who died for our sakes. The cross acquires a religious cultic significance and Jesus' death becomes an act of communication with God, "to bring repentance to Israel and forgiveness of sins." Jesus died as "a ransom for many," whose shedding of blood expiates sins. Jesus gave himself for a purpose. His death was an outpouring of love. From a negative event, the cross acquires a positive meaning.

In the course of time and movement across cultures, the positive meanings of Jesus' death became lost or distorted. In the Philippines, we have developed (or inherited) a dead-end theology of the cross with no resurrection or salvation in sight. Most of the women who sing the "pasyon" during Holy Week look upon the passion and death of Jesus as ends in themselves and actually relish being victims. This attitude is not uncommon among other women outside the "pasyon" singers, and it is not helped when priests reinforce the attitude through their homilies. One of them said not long ago that he does not preach the resurrection as "the people are not prepared for it."

In India, the theology of sacrifice thrust upon women is of no purpose. Indian women theologians[7] tell us that their women silently bear taunts, abuse, and even battering; they sacrifice their self-esteem for the sake of family honor, subject themselves to sex determination tests, and endure the oppressive and even fatal effects of the dowry system. A woman who is raped will invariably commit suicide rather than allow her husband and family to suffer the ignominy of living with a raped woman. While we seek in Jesus' passion, death, and resurrection a meaning for our own suffering, we cannot passively submit ourselves as women to practices that are ultimately anti-life. Only that suffering endured for the sake of one's neighbor, for the sake of the kingdom, for the sake of greater life, can be redeeming and rooted in the Paschal mystery.

The death of Jesus was not only a redeeming event; it was also revelatory. In Jesus' death, God revealed the deepest meaning and extent of divine love for humankind as well as the true nature of God. Jesus' whole life was a disclosure of God and God's will for humankind. He always felt a deep communion and intimate relationship with God which was manifested in his being and in his prayer. It was only on the cross that he felt abandoned by this very God whom he called Abba—"Father." But God was both absent and present on the cross. "On the cross of Jesus God himself is crucified...In this ultimate solidarity with humanity, he reveals himself as the God of love, who opens up a hope and a future through the most negative side of history."[8]

IV

The nature of Jesus' relationship to God was only reflected upon and gradually formulated after the resurrection. At first it was simply the application of the biblical titles to Jesus in the light of the resurrection experience: the Christ, Son of Man, Suffering Servant, Son of God, Lord, Son of David. Initially functional, the designations gradually took on a confessional dimension. Eventually, with increasing association with the Hellenistic world, ontological implications were drawn out. Thus through a process of historical growth and theological development, the identity of Jesus in terms of divinity was recognized and accepted by the early church, paving the way for the doctrine of the Incarnation, the doctrine of the Word made flesh.

Whether Jesus is true God and true man, or only seemingly God or only seemingly man, became the subject of intensive debates that were dogmatically put to a halt by the authoritative formulations of the Council of Nicea (325 C.E.) and later the Council of Chalcedon (451 C.E.), asserting that Jesus Christ is fully divine of one substance with God the Father (Nicea), the same perfect in his divinity and the same perfect in his humanity, one and the same Christ, Lord, only begotten, in two natures (Chalcedon).[9] The language and substance of these christological doctrines betray their historical and cultural conditionings, addressing as they did the disputes of another time and place which do not relate to the vital problems of present-day Asia. These doctrines are no longer of the greatest importance for many Asian theologians, for taken as they are, they close off any authentic dialogue with people of other faiths, who are the vast majority in Asia. In fact, in one Asian theologian's view,[10] christology has become passé in Asia, because we are still depending on Nicea and Chalcedon whose formulations are largely unintelligible to the Asian mind. Thus the true significance of these councils is not so much their content, but the underlying challenge they pose to us to have our own contemporary culturally-based christological formulations. And that is what small groups of Asian theologians, both men and women, are doing— having their own mini and informal Niceas and Chalcedons to determine, based on their context and concerns, who Jesus Christ is for them.

Just as the formulations of Nicea and Chalcedon have placed barriers in our efforts to have an honest dialogue with people of other faiths, so have our claims about Jesus as the universal savior. In Asia we experience dialogue on two levels, a more formal one commonly referred to as "interreligious dialogue" and a less formal one we refer to as "dialogue of life." Our experience in the latter where we share the life conditions, pain, risks, struggles, and aspirations of the Asian poor (majority of whom are of other faiths or even of "no faith") has made us aware of our common search for a truly human life, our common desire for liberation from whatever shackles us internally and externally, and our common thrust towards a just society reflective of what we Christians term "the kingdom." In the struggle that binds us, there is an implicit acknowledgment and acceptance of our religious differences and our different paths to "salvation."

On the more formal level, Asian theologians engaged in authentic interreligious dialogue (which has mutual enlightenment and not conversion as goal) are explicitly questioning our traditional claims about the uniqueness and centrality of Jesus and the universality of Jesus as savior...for all religions. Biblical and historical research and in-depth study of other religions have raised serious questions about our Christian claims. Admitting God's universal love and desire to save, the Catholic position recognizes both revelation and salvation outside Christ and Christianity, but insists that Christ be proclaimed as "the unique mediator of salvation" and God's "unique historical revelation."[11] But is it not possible to claim Jesus Christ as "our" unique savior without claiming the same for all other people? The present direction toward theocentric or soteriocentric christologies seem to be where some Asian theologians are tending as a result of their experience of dialogue, encounter, study and reflection. Jesus himself centered on God and the kingdom and not on himself. As an old saying goes: let us not take the finger pointing at the moon to be the moon itself.

Theologians proclaiming that Jesus is wholly God but not the whole of God, or that Jesus is the Christ but the Christ is not Jesus,[12] should in no way lessen our own personal commitment to Jesus whom we Christians have personally known and experienced as revealer, savior, truth, way, and life. It should in no way disaffirm for us that the "vision and power of Jesus of Nazareth is an effective, hope-filled, universally meaningful way of bringing about God's kingdom."[13] We believe and confess that Jesus has brought us total salvation; others, however, are making similar claims about their own mediators with the same Ultimate Source of life's meaning whom we call God.

V

I shall now examine some implications of my christology for certain aspects of Christian practice, including the use of Jesus images. In particular, I shall reflect on its implications for mission ministry.

From the start, though I set out to write a christology I can claim as mine, I have tried to keep in mind the plight, concerns, and aspirations of my Asian sisters. In the light of Asian women's reality in general, a liberational, hope-filled, love-inspired, and praxis-oriented christology is what holds meaning for me. In the person and praxis of Jesus are found the grounds of our liberation from all oppression and discrimination: whether political or economic, religious or cultural, or based on gender, race or ethnicity. Therefore the image of Jesus as liberator is consistent with my christology. On the other hand, in view of what I have written, it would be inconsistent to hold on to the title and image of "lord" in reference to Jesus, because of the overtones of the word as used today. In Asia, the word "lord" is connected with the feudal system which in my own country is one of the root causes of the poverty, injustices, inequalities, and violent conflicts that exist there today, many of the victims being women. It is also a colonial term for the British masters which is still used in countries like Pakistan for those who have taken their place. "Lord" connotes a relationship of domination, which is opposite to what Jesus taught and exemplified. "The rulers of the gentiles exercise lordship over them...but not so with you" (Lk 22:24). His apostles called him "teacher" and "lord," yet Jesus preferred to be remembered as one who serves (cf Jn 14:13-16). Asian women have been "lorded over" for centuries and all the major religions including Christianity have contributed to this sinful situation. The title "lord" would not be in keeping with a liberating Jesus.

In my own culture, however, not many women would be familiar with the figure of a liberating or liberated Jesus. They know him as the suffering or crucified Jesus who understands their own suffering which they passively or resignedly endure. Many remain unaware of their class and gender oppression and simply live on with a "status quo" christology. Nevertheless, an increasing number of women are becoming aware of our subordinate place and exploited state in a patriarchal church and society, and see this as contrary to the will of a just and loving God, who created both men and women in God's own image. As these women strive to change this inequitable situation within the overall struggle against economic, political and social injustices, they, too, see Jesus as their hope and liberator.

In our quest for a world of right human relationships, Jesus has shown us the way, and therefore Jesus is the norm for our action in reforming our lives and renewing society. Jesus never spoke of human rights or the common good or liberation from oppressive structures, yet his whole life, teachings and actions embodied all of them, manifesting what it meant to be human and to act humanly. He showed us that we cannot work toward our true humanity, our true liberation, unless we seek the true humanity, the true liberation, of all. Thus, efforts to transform the existing structures and patterns of domination that prevent the least of our sisters and brothers from living truly human lives and enjoying just, reciprocal relationships, are moral actions.

Just as my christology has implications for ethics, so it has implications for ecclesiology and my sense of anthropology and culture. In relation to ecclesiology, I have already mentioned that the present Catholic model admits the possibility of salvation beyond the borders of Christianity. God loves and wills the salvation of all humankind. Thus the church can claim to be *a* sign but not, as Vatican II put it, *"the* sign of salvation for the entire world (*underlining mine*)."[14] There are other fingers pointing at the same moon. The Church needs to reexamine its sense of "uniqueness" and "universality." Also, if its dialogue with other religions is to be serious and sincere, then it must reexamine its meaning and use of "definitiveness" and "normativeness."

To be a credible sign of salvation and to witness to Jesus' universal love, the Church as institution has to rid itself of its non-liberating structures and non-loving practices, its exclusive, hierarchical mode of operation. It would do well to retrieve the egalitarian spirit of the early Christian communities. Unfortunately some of today's new experiences of being community are construed as a threat by the institutional Church, instead of as an attempt to live out that spirit which grew from a faithful following of Jesus. If the Church is indeed following in the steps of Jesus, then it should focus, as Jesus did, on preaching and living out the truths of the kingdom rather than in maintaining itself. If the Church is serious in following Jesus, then it should encourage and support all efforts towards inclusiveness and full humanity.

Jesus intended this full humanity for all, not just for men, or less for women. Men and women have the same human nature and are endowed with the same potentials for "fullness." Men do not image God more than women do. Yet patriarchy has distorted these truths to promote a hierarchical and complementary model of humanity, which puts women in second place. Women's inferior status has become part of the working definition of being human in Asia, buttressed by the doctrines and practices of the major religions. This has had degrading and dehumanizing consequences for women in all areas of life down the ages, stark evidences of which are still present on our continent today. One of the deplorable consequences is the very internalization of this "ideology" of women's inferiority by women themselves as part and parcel of our cultures. Part of the work of an Asian christology would be to determine the emancipating and enslaving elements of cultures and religions, to discern which ones foster and which ones impede the creation of a more human and humane life and a more just society.

VI

Lastly, there are certain implications of my christology for mission ministry. The understanding of mission has undergone changes over the years and especially of late when the church has been present in almost all parts of the world. Transmission of the message in a transcultural milieu has acquired new modalities.[15] Besides direct evangelization, missionaries are engaged in other activities: "witness" on behalf of the Gospel, "prophetic" communication in word and sign, and involvement in personal and social transformation.

Throughout the past centuries, there has been such an urgency about planting the Church that in preaching Jesus Christ, the stress has been given to the Church he "founded" and its doctrine rather than the reign of God he proclaimed. Indeed, if our mission is an extension of Jesus' own mission, then we need to refocus on preaching the good news of God (Mk 1:14) and God's reign which Jesus has already inaugurated and will come in its fullness in the future as God's gift. Jesus' message of salvation was not only preached, but also actualized as something to be experienced in this life. To make Jesus' message comprehensible to Asians (its core and not its cultural overlays), we Christians need to engage in sincere and humble dialogue with people of other faiths, a dialogue which is as open to receive as to give, that in so doing we ourselves may come to grasp a fuller meaning of God's revelation. To make Jesus' message credible to Asian women, it must directly touch their everyday lives. Interreligious dialogue that is silent on women's oppression and thus simply perpetuating their subordinate status in religion and society is contrary to Jesus' saving word.

Our witness is for the sake of the good news of God's reign; the good news is not just to be preached but lived. Thus our life and work style must conform to the kingdom norms and values. We cannot proclaim a reign of justice, love and peace, while at the same time contradicting its inclusive, non-dominating character in our mission practice and structures. If the kingdom is our focus, then a more collaborative, egalitarian, ecumenical effort in mission will be a more compelling witness.

Some missionaries will be called to prophetic witness, which is not only to announce the liberating message of Jesus but, in solidarity with the people, to denounce what is incompatible with it. This requires both prayerful discernment and courage. New styles of mission presence will indeed create misunderstanding and provoke resistance, not only from outside but within the church itself. But suffering and even persecution are to be expected in a missionary's life if indeed it follows the path of Jesus. Suffering for the sake of God's reign is a way of being in mission.

While many mission societies still insist on the primacy of first evangelization in mission, others have moved on to works of inculturation and liberation, both urgent tasks in Asia. While these are primarily the tasks of Asians themselves, they invite the support and collaboration of others, and missionaries have responded to this invitation. Missionaries are taking seriously what the Synod of Bishops said in 1971, that the mission of preaching the gospel demands our participation in the transformation of the world.[16] Thus active solidarity with the people against sexism, racism, ethnic discrimination and economic injustice is truly missionary. For women missionaries all over the world, there is need to explore new mission ministries among, and on behalf of, women who need other women's support, presence, defense, sisterly help, friendship and active solidarity as they awaken to their reality and struggle for their full humanity. In Asia these women are numberless.

I have reflected on the significance of Jesus' life, death, and resurrection from a specific horizon. It was my concern, however, that my christology not only express who Jesus is for me, but also recapture Jesus' life and message in such a way that it can be liberating and empowering for other women. Hopefully my christology will form part of the collective effort of Asian Christian women in search of a christology that is meaningful not only to us but to our Asian sisters whose life's struggles we have made our own. For now this is what I submit as my christology as an Asian woman, knowing that it is subject to additions and revisions, and aware of the fact that the task of christology is ongoing and never really finished.

NOTES

1. "Proceedings of the Asian Women's Consultation," Manila, Philippines, November 21-30, 1985. Mimeographed.

2. Rosemary Radford Ruether, "Feminist Theology and Spirituality," in *Christian Feminism: Vision of a New Humanity,* ed. Judith L. Weidman (San Francisco: Harper & Row, Publishers, 1984), 20.

3. Some Asian women question this claim as coming from a male perspective. What Asian women need liberation from is not inordinate greed but excessive self-effacement.

4. cf. Aloysius Pieris, "Speaking of the Son of God in *Non-Christian* Cultures, e.g. in Asia," in Jesus, Son of God, *Concilium* 153, eds. E. Schillebeeckx and J.B. Metz (New York: Seabury Press, 1982), 65-70; "To Be Poor As Jesus Was Poor," *The Way,* 24, no.3 (July 1984) 186-197; and "Spirit Dimension of Change," *The Way,* 28/1 (January 1988): 36-37.

5. George M. Soares, interview by author, 5 December 1987, New Delhi, India.

6. Paul's claim to be an apostle because he had seen the risen Jesus and received a direct commission to preach the good news applies equally to Mary Magdalene (cf.John 20:16-18).

7. "Proceedings of the Asian Women's Consulation," 54-55.

8. Jon Sobrino, *Christology at the Crossroads* (Maryknoll, New York: Orbis Books, 1978), 224.

9. Dermot A. Lane, *The Reality of Jesus* (New York: Paulist Press, 1975), 99, 105.

10. Francis D'Sa, interview by author, 5 December 1987, New Delhi, India.

11. R. Hardawiryana, "Towards a 'Theology in Asia':The Struggle for Identity," *Inter-Religio* 12 (Fall 1987): 52-53.

12. Paul F. Knitter, *No Other Name?* (Maryknoll, New York: Orbis Books, 1986), 152, 156.

13. Ibid., 196.

14. Cited in ibid., 130.

15. Donald Senior and Carroll Stuhlmueller, *The Biblical Foundations for Mission* (Maryknoll, New York: Orbis Books, 1983), 332-339 passim.

16. Synod of Bishops 1971, "Justice in the World," in *Renewing the Earth,* eds. David J. O'Brien and Thomas A. Shannon (Garden City, New York: Image Books, 1977), 391.

2

Christology and Women

Monica Melanchton (India)

Christology is in itself a very large subject and I am not rash enough to imagine that any one paper can cover it adequately or comprehensively. The task is all the more difficult when one has to discuss it in the light of its meaning and significance for women, for until now tradition has said very little or probably nothing at all in this connection. The time has now come for us women to make some genuine attempts at new thinking and work freshly with new ideas in order to represent traditional christological affirmations in a manner that is meaningful and relevant to our context and, more important, inclusive of women. This means a constant awareness of past and present attitudes which have been or are still wounding or deforming. [1] Such a task requires courage but we move on in hope that things will be different when we attempt new things.

Christology or the doctrine of Christ is the enquiry into the significance of Jesus for Christian faith. But then who is Jesus? In the New Testament, the writers indicate who Jesus is by describing the significance of the work he came to do and the office he came to fulfill. These varied descriptions of his work and office based on the Old Testament always blend with one another and enrich one another without negating any of the earlier traditions. The humanity of Jesus Christ is taken for granted in the Synoptic Gospels. We see him lying in the manger, growing, learning, feeling the pangs of hunger and thirst, having emotions as anxiety, doubt, grief and finally dying and being buried. But elsewhere his humanity is witnessed to as if it might be called into question or its significance neglected.[2]

Besides this emphasis on his true humanity, there is nevertheless always an emphasis on the fact that even in his humanity he is sinless and also utterly different from all of humankind. The virgin birth and the resurrection are signs that we have someone unique in the realm of humanity. Who he is and what he is can be discovered only by contrasting him with others and this shines out most clearly when the others are against him.[3] The tremendous authority Jesus claimed and exercised was outside the possibility of any human teacher. The thing that impressed the masses was that the teaching of Jesus was differentiated from that of the Scribes by its innate sense of authority. It was with this power vested in him that he exorcised, forgave sins, healed the sick and preached with authority. That any mere human could claim such authority and back it up with his actions is beyond the remotest possibility.[4] Hence every New Testament book attributes divinity to Jesus either by direct statement or by inference.

The Christian tradition has long held that we can understand who Jesus is only by looking at his whole life and activity. Recent theology has stressed this inseparability of the person and work of Christ. The human life and teaching of the historical Jesus have to be given full place in his saving work as essential and not incidental or merely instrumental in his reconciliation. Here we must give due weight to modern biblical study in helping us to realise both what kind of a man Jesus was and yet also to see this Jesus of history as the Christ of faith, the Lord, the Son of God.

The entire life of Jesus must therefore be the subject of our investigation. It follows that any attempt to fathom the significance of that life must look at it as a whole because we do not know what is important and what is not. Christianity is a historical faith; thus the history of the life of its founder is of supreme importance. There can be no adequate christology except that which is based on the life of Jesus the Christ. Through the study of his office and work we come to understand how his humanity is not only truly individual but also representative.

Modern theological discussions continue to be a witness to the centrality of Jesus Christ in the matters of faith. The Gospels do provide us with sufficient historical details about Jesus. The importance of regaining such genuine understanding of his humanity as a basis for our christology has been stressed.

Theology has always been dynamic and the fluid nature of christological thought indicates that women too, like the liberation theologians of Asia and Latin America, can also interpret the doctrine of Christ within a specified frame of reference which is meaningful to us as women. The frame of reference used by classical dogma is no longer adequate and hence the many changes in christological thought.[5]

This paper will not attempt to outline the history of christological thought or the positions taken by the many early church fathers or modern theologians or go into the intricacies of christological debate. Rather it will work on two basic christological affirmations and their significance for Indian women. The two christological affirmations are: (1) the human and divine nature of Jesus Christ, and (2) his redemptive work extended to all human beings both men and women.

I

The union of two natures in one person has been a source of endless difficulty in the history of the Church. It would appear that there are two primary sources of such difficulty. One of these is an emphasis on a part of the New Testament record to the exclusion of another part. A second is the inability of the finite human mind to comprehend the infinite.[6] It is important that we avoid the following kinds of errors:[7] (1) confusion of two natures so that the resultant personality is neither human nor divine; (2) separation of the two natures so as to give Jesus a double or split personality; (3) emphasizing his divinity so as to exclude his humanity; and (4) emphasizing his humanity so as to exclude the deity. Loranie Boettner describes the relation of the two natures in the following words:

> Throughout the whole study of the relationship which exists between the two natures we are, of course, face to face with impenetrable mystery. It is one of those mysteries which the Scriptures reveal but which they make no effort to explain. Christ is in an absolutely unique person, and although in every age much study has been expended upon his personality it remains a profound mystery, in some respects as baffling as the Trinity itself. All we can know are the simple facts which are revealed to us in Scripture, and beyond these it is not necessary to go. As a matter of fact we do not understand the mysterious union of the spiritual and physical in our own nature, nor do we understand the attributes of God. But the essential facts are clear and understandable by the average Christian. These are, that the second Person of the Trinity added to His own nature a perfectly normal human nature, that His life on earth was passed as far as was fitting within the limits of this humanity, that His life remained at all times the life of God manifest in the flesh, that His action in the flesh never escaped beyond the boundary of that which was suitable for the incarnate Deity, and that all of this was done in order that in man's and as man's Substitute He might assume man's obligation before the law, suffer the penalty which was due to him for sin, and so accomplish his redemption.[8]

The above description of the relation between the two natures can be accepted without any question as long as the term, 'man' in the quote includes both the male and female members of the community. The problem arises for women when this doctrine of Christ is distorted and particularised. Women are deprived fuller participation in the life of the Church because the Church assumes a christological premise which declares that Jesus as male was a necessary precondition of Christ's being what he was and doing what he did.[9] In other words the reality of God-with-us is such that the natural means of its actualisation is a male human being.[10]

But "in God's togetherness with us, particular people and events become the bearers of meaning, not only because of but in spite of, their concrete particularity in the history of one small group of people, or one wandering Jewish rabbi"[11] —Jesus. But neither the Jewishness of Jesus or his physical presence in the first century in community is particularised, only his maleness. His maleness, by being particularised, is used to keep women away from ordination and meaningful participation in the life of the Church and community. Therefore, in christology a new enquiry is needed towards understan-

17

ding the relationship of the historical Jesus of Nazareth to the risen Christ of faith. The maleness of the historical Jesus is a matter of past record, but does this mean that the resurrected Christ in the redeemed order of creation is identified with the male principle? The fact is that the resurrected Christ who transcended all particularities is forgotten and the male historical Jesus is remembered. The argument put forward is simply that Jesus was a male. And no one questions that.

It is further argued that Jesus was also the bearer of God's salvation and Emmanuel—'God with us'; hence his maleness becomes a constitutive factor in deciding the place and the role of women. How is it that the maleness of Jesus defines the roles of both men and women when he represents only the male half of the human race? This is a question that is not answered by those who oppose the participation of women in the Church. Some have wondered if it is necessary for women to look for another representative of new humanity. But we cannot do so because as Christian women we have affirmed Christ to be the subject of Christian theology,[12] and therefore the problem of Jesus' maleness continues to exist. If women take Christ to be the representative of new humanity, it is the task of women to assert and emphasize the humanness of Jesus, rather than his maleness.

It can be assumed that classical tradition has never spoken of the maleness of Jesus because it did not consider it to be important or significant,[13] though it did accord christological significance to characteristics such as obedience, faith, love, concern and so on which are not male characteristics but human characteristics.[14] Therefore, if we accept the maleness of Jesus as an argument against the ordination of women, we are in fact not only distorting the doctrine of Christ but also altering tradition.[15] Besides, the argument is an affront to women because it gives one the idea that salvation is only for men through Jesus the male. Therefore we women who believe otherwise need to be very careful in our interpretation of the doctrine of Christ.

When the church Fathers speak of the incarnation of the divine *logos,* they speak in terms which emphasize his participation in the general human condition. The beginnings of such a thought is found in the New Testament itself. The divine Son became 'flesh' (Jn 1:14), he assumed 'the form of a slave' (Phil 2:7), and 'tasted death' (Heb 2:9) on behalf of all human beings. Such expressions as these not only point to the natural characteristics of Jesus, but also to the fact that in him the Divine Word accepted the limitations, the weakness and the suffering which are the common lot of humanity, whether Jewish or Greek or male or female.[16]

Later Christian writers such as Ignatius of Antioch and Justin Martyr stressed the importance of the Divine Word in human finitude. They used terms such as fleshness, createdness, birth, death, to explain the Greek term *anthropos,* meaning 'human person', as opposed to divine beings.[17] What is important christologically about the humanity of Jesus is not its Jewishness, maleness, or any other such characteristic but simply the fact that he was like his brothers and sisters in every respect.

Even in the time when christological controversies began, the church Fathers felt it necessary to emphasize the humanity of Jesus—its wholeness and inclusiveness. The Greek term *anthropos* is equivalent to the Johannine term, 'flesh' (Jn 1:1). A deeper study into the writings of the early church Fathers reveals to us the fact that neither the Jewishness nor the maleness was important, but rather the understanding that the Incarnation was the "likeness of the word of God in his humanity to all those who are included within the scope of his redemption."[18] And we believe that women are also included in this act of redemption. To make of the maleness of Christ a christological principle is to deny the university of Christ's redemption.[19]

There are those who argue, however, that Jesus' maleness is somehow intrinsic to his character as God-with-us. Christian theology, grounding itself in the New Testament, has always spoken of the relation between the first and the second Persons of the Trinity in term of Fatherhood and Sonship. But the supposition that God the Father shares the biological characteristics of human males who procreate sons is a travesty of the doctrine.[20] Jesus' designation of God as 'Father' and the Old Testament concept of divine fatherhood is only based on an intimate level of relationship, the trustworthiness and authority of the deity, but *not* upon a supposed masculinity of God. Addressing God as 'Abba' is only indicative of a kind of relationship. God is not father in the physical sexual sense in which a male human being is a father. Divine fatherhood is neither sexual nor sexist in the New Testament or the Old Testament. To use the New Testament references to the fatherhood of God in an attempt to prove God's maleness is to wrench the New Testament material from its grounding in the Old Testament principle of God's sexual transcendence and to graft it on to "pagan" notions about the sexuality of the Deity.[21]

Theology employs symbolisms and anthropomorphisms which are mere accommodations to human speech. Maleness is one of the features of human fatherhood which cannot be attributed to God. The same should be said of femaleness. To ignore this is to interpret the biblical imagery in a way that is inconsistent with the intention of the Hebrew writers. Thus, it must be said that from both a christological and theological perspective, the fact of Jesus' maleness is not a constitutive factor in the meaning of 'God-with-us'. Neither is maleness constitutive of Jesus as the Christ. On the contrary, christology envisages Jesus as the representative human being—a category which includes female human beings.

II

The women in the Indian Church are no better off than they are in the society at large. The many problems that affect the lives of women in society are also existent in the Church. This is because the social customs and traditions prevalent in society have seeped into Church structures and into the minds of the members of the Church, thereby smothering and distorting the intentions of God for women as written in Scriptures. The Indian society, which is hierarchical and male-dominated, thrives on a system that is detrimental to the growth and wholesome development of a person, especially a woman. The Indian woman is socially dependent on a male. She lives in an ethos that is stifling; at every stage in her life she has to face many odds.

The Christian population in India is only 2.8 percent of the total population and it is mostly urban and semi-urban. As said earlier, the secondary position assigned to women in the Churches is supported by existent cultural and social norms. Moreover, Christian women are weighed down by wrongly interpreted, or selective use of, biblical passages.

The Protestant Churches in India are separate and independent, differing in traditions, cultural norms, theological positions and patterns of worship. They also have different mission boards. The position of women is different in each Church though one can discern commonalities and similarities. Only churches such as the Church of South India, the Church of North India and the Methodist Church in India ordain women, while it is still under discussion in the Lutheran Church in India. For the Marthoma and Syrian Orthodox women there is still a long way to go before we can see results.

There is an increasing number of women pursuing theological education, and many of them without any Church support or sponsorship. Most of them have to go through the additional burden of hunting for a job after the completion of their studies. They often work in low-paying and stereotyped jobs. Many of the women workers in the Church are supported by the women's wing of the Church who have to raise the money to pay these women; yet most of these women's groups give a regular contribution to the Church bursary. In spite of a significant number of theologically-trained women present in India, the number of women in theological faculties is not worth mentioning. The few that are on theological faculties teach mostly in the departments of English or Christian education.

The Church in India needs to come to terms with the fact that it has erected many barriers against a fuller and more meaningful participation of women. The walls of hostility between the sexes need to be broken down and a new community built on oneness and love which we experience in our faith in Jesus the Christ. The doctrine of Christ—his personhood, in which we believe, and the universality of Christ's redemption—should be the ground on which we build our faith. The Church in India needs to recognise the personhood of Jesus Christ and the fact that Christ is the representative human being for all people including Indian women.

III

In the introductory section of this paper, it was mentioned that we can understand who Jesus is only by looking at his whole life and activity. There is an increasing stress being laid on this inseparability of the person and work of Jesus the Christ. The redemptive work of Christ included both men and women. This is seen clearly in the many incidents recorded in the Bible where Jesus pays special attention to women, more so in a time when the predominant religion, Judaism, influenced the society at large to have a fairly low view of women. It is a fact that Jesus was good to women. Jesus took women seriously, ministered to their needs, challenged them to go beyond their ideas of themselves. He showed, in fact, just the same attitude to women as to men. But reaching out to women in the manner that he did was beyond the customary norms of acceptable Jewish male behaviour.

Over and over again, the great truths about Jesus are revealed to and accepted by women. At a time when Samaritans were looked down upon, Jesus spoke to a Samaritan, and a woman besides, and drank the water which she drew from the well. He declared to her that he was the Christ. He engaged himself in a theological discourse with this Samaritan woman at a time when theology was considered of no use to women (Jn 4:7ff). He forgave the woman caught in adultery who was condemned alone for an act that involves a man and woman (Jn 8:3ff). He healed the woman who was bent and publicly called her a "daughter of Abraham," thereby asserting the act that she too was by right a part of the covenant relationship that God had made with Abraham (Lk 13:10ff). He healed the woman suffering for years with the issue of blood (Mt 9:20ff). He addressed a woman who was considered unclean as "daughter." He upheld the poor widow who gave the little she had as offering to God, as the right model for his disciples (Mk 12:41ff). Jesus showed mercy on the woman whose daughter was possessed by a demon and healed her daughter (Mt 15:21ff). Jesus showed love, respect and honour to women. This has sometimes been misinterpreted as pity or condescending male benevolence to helpless, sinful and ignorant women. But this is a gross misrepresentation. Jesus' concern for women was genuine, filled with understanding of their plight in a society that was male-dominated and therefore oppressive with its double standard.

Though Jesus had no women among the chosen twelve, the discipleship of women comes to the fore through their faith statements and presence during the time of the passion and the resurrection. In John 11:12 we see that Martha receives the knowledge of Jesus' life-giving power and professes her belief in him as the Christ. It was the women who stayed at his side when he was on the cross and who were the first witnesses to his resurrection, though they are not given credit for it. Women entered into faith in Jesus on exactly the same basis as the men who followed him. Both men and women need to work with equal fervour and devotion and exertion to become part of and share in the faith. The one thing necessary is commitment.

The Indian society is not very different from the Judeo-Roman world of Jesus. Women are considered to be inferior and evil and therefore second class citizens. The Indian social structures and institutions like the caste system and the religious values and practices all consolidate women's subordinate position.

India is a land of many peoples and religions. Within each religion there are many sects and they teach the subjugation of women in their own way.

The government of India, because it is a secular state respecting all religions, honors the personal laws of each religion, even if these laws are not only discriminating but have a deep-rooted prejudice against women. Furthermore, these religions sanction some of the evil practices against women such as dowry, the devadasi* system, sati*, etc. (*devadasi = temple Prostitution; *sati = widows being burnt on the funeral pyre of their husbands).

There is a continuous decline in the sex ratio in India due to the high female mortality rate. This is due not only to improper medical care and unavailability of sufficient medical facilities, but also to the increase in the number of abortions when the feotus is known to be female. If a female survives all this, from the time of birth, the child is condemned to a life of subjugation and suppression. Because of the dowry system, there is discrimination against, and neglect of, female children.

The majority of the women are illiterate and economically dependent on the man in the family. Most of the employed women work in the unorganised and unskilled sector or in the agricultural fields. Their wages are low because they are unorganised and unskilled. Their jobs are insecure as they can be sacked at any time without reason. Their working condition is not good; they often have to face sexual and physical harassment in the workplace.

Politically they are unaware and ignorant of the political climate of the country. This arises out of the feeling that politics is not women's business. Often they vote for the person whom their husbands have selected. Most women are ignorant of the fact that before the law all citizens, male and female, are equal. Women are not aware of their legal status or the many existent laws pertaining to women and their rights. They do not make use of the provisions that the law offers them. But this does not mean that the law is perfect for it has many loopholes which an incompetent lawyer might overlook.

Besides this, in the private sphere, women are raped within and outside marriage, deserted, sold, burnt, and battered physically, emotionally and psychologically. Victims of premarital pregnancy are stigmatised; widows are filled with a feeling of remorse when they are ill-treated because they are considered unclean and a bad omen; many welcome death as a release and many commit suicide. Victims of rape are offered no emotional or physical support and have to suffer social stigma for the rest of their lives. Widow remarriage is frowned upon and the morality of the woman who remarries is questioned. A divorcee is treated with suspicion. The plight of women in India is really pathetic.

As Christians and imitators of Christ, we in the Church need to overcome the existent sexist biases and work towards the full incorporation of women into the life of the Church. Jesus did not ignore women but took them into his fold and made certain that the men around him were aware of it. As the representative of all human beings, his saving acts were extended to all, both male and female. That was his mission on earth and if we want to be a part of his faith and partners with him in carrying out the task of salvation, the evil practices against women have to stop. Women have to be recognised as equals, as co-workers, with a sense of dignity and worth.

In India, as in many other countries, religion plays a very important role in the lives of the people. In fact, it is religion that undergirds our thinking, influences our behaviour, develops our value system, and determines our relationship with others. It is therefore very important not to undermine the role that religion plays, and to be careful in our interpretation of Scriptural passages, the formulation of our theology and the articulation of our faith. The right interpretation of the person and work of Christ, the basis of our Christian faith, the very core of our religion, is something very necessary and urgent for this gives meaning to our lives.

Christ is the one in whom all things are summed up (Eph 1:10). The recognition of this truth will enable a fuller participation of women, and this fuller participation of women in turn represents a Church and society expressive of Christ the Divine *Logos*, who became flesh in order to bring salvation to all.

NOTES

1. M. Furlong, ed., *Feminine in the Church* (London: SPCK, 1984), 1.
2. A. Richardson, ed., *Dictionary of Christian Theology.* See "Christology."
3. Ibid.
4. C.C. Anderson, *The Historical Jesus: A Continuing Quest* (Grand Rapids: Eerdmans Publishing Co., 1972), 24.
5. A.Richardson, *Dictionary of Christian Theology.*
6. C.C. Anderson, *The Historical Jesus,* 24.
7. Ibid.
8. Loranie Boettner, *Studies in Theology* (Grand Rapids: Eerdmans Publishing Co., 1947), 202-203.
9. M. Furlong, *Feminine in the Church,* 72.
10. Ibid.
11. Letty M. Russell, *Human Liberation in a Feminist Perspective—A Theology* (Philadelphia: The Westminster Press, 1974), 33-135.
12. Ibid.
13. M. Furlong, *Feminine in the Church,* 76.
14. Ibid.
15. Ibid.
16. Ibid.
17. Ibid.
18. M. Furlong, *Feminine in the Church,* 78.
19. Ibid.
20. M. Hayter, *The New Eve in Christ* (London: SPCK, 1987), 35.
21. Ibid.

3

Ecclesiology and Women:
A View from Taiwan

Lily Kuo Wang (Taiwan)

The subject of this paper is "Women and the Church." My primary purpose in writing this paper is to better understand my own situation as a woman pastor of the Presbyterian Church in Taiwan. The subject is quite broad, and so I have chosen to limit "Women and the Church" in the following way. First I shall describe the position of women in the Presbyterian Church of my own country, Taiwan, the Republic of China. I shall include women's social and cultural background, a review of Presbyterian outreach for women, and also the current situation of women within my church. Then I shall consider the early church as described in the New Testament, both in its qualities and in its structure. "How did women belong?" shall be the question I shall try to answer in the next section. I will conclude this paper with suggestions on how the Presbyterian Church in Taiwan could make specific improvements in order to provide encouragement and opportunities for its women.

WOMEN IN THE TAIWANESE CHURCH

Traditionally, in Taiwan society, women had no status. Instead, they were regarded as the property of men and at best, their subordinate. From childhood, both men and women were educated in this way; no one was able to think otherwise. Women were expected to keep silent in public. At home, they could not eat with the men. Their work was limited to housework; therefore, it was thought that women had no need for formal education. On the whole, women were treated as non-persons.

However, women's situation began to change 120 years ago when missionaries first brought the Gospel to Taiwan. Christianity began to break down the traditional attitude toward women and the unfair practices. The Christians emphasized the need for women's education, and several schools were established especially for girls and women. One of these specialized in teaching "Bible Women" who served as evangelists and lay pastors in the growing church. In 1922 the Women's Home Mission Society was established. These women were very active in Bible studies, teacher training, and setting up local women's circles in congregations. About 1950 women were accepted for the ordination to the gospel ministry, as well as to serve as elders and deacons. Today there are more than seventy women who have graduated from the Presbyterian seminaries, representing ten percent of the graduates. Of these, twenty-two women have been ordained as Presbyterian ministers.

In 1981 the Association of Theologically Trained Women in Taiwan was begun. This group, made up of Presbyterian Church leaders, meet three times a year for Bible study, discussion and training on women's issues, and mutual sharing. As a special project they sponsor teams to do evangelism among the mountain churches.

Although in the last forty years there have been many opportunities for women to minister in the church, there are still many obstacles. Many men are still unable to accept women in the church in leadership positions. Why is this so? Men are concerned that a woman living alone in a church would not be safe. Also the male sense of superiority remains in their minds, so they cannot accept a woman minister in charge who would have authority over them. Male deacons and elders in particular feel that a woman's authority is inappropriate.

A woman minister I know said, "Women often meet the challenges before them as pastors. They have the knowledge, the skills and the abilities to be good pastors. The problem lies with the local church. Is the local church willing to accept a woman as its pastor? Most people, when they see a woman minister, think that this is a very strange thing! They feel that a woman, compared to a man, lacks the proper ability. Actually it doesn't matter if we are male or female, our job is to share the gospel. So I wish to encourage more and more women to enter the pastoral ministry because there is much work to be done."

THE NEW TESTAMENT CHURCH

We can approach the early church, as described in the New Testament, from several different directions. About the early church we may ask questions beginning with "what, where, why, how, when, who"; and all of the answers would be important. Yet I want to emphasize just two of these questions, "Who is the early church?" Or, what was their self-concept, their calling? Also we will consider, "How was the early church structured?" How did the church live out the practical, everyday reality of authority and work? How did they provide for their continuity? Then with both of these questions we shall ask, "How did women belong?"

If we could ask the members of one or more of the early churches, "Who are you?'' how would they respond? From the letters of Paul we can affirm these answers.

We are sanctified, we are justified. The existence of the church is dependent upon God's active love and grace. Through Jesus Christ and the Holy Spirit, Christians may receive God's gracious gifts. Sanctification means that we are becoming more and more the image of Christ; we are becoming holy and perfect; we are being changed into Christ's likeness. "But you were washed, you were sanctified, you were justified in the name of the Lord Jesus Christ and in the Spirit of our God" (1Cor 6:11). Justification means that we have been saved from death and destruction through the death of Jesus Christ. "For the law of the Spirit of life in Christ Jesus has set me free from the law of sin and death" (Rom 8:2).

We are believers and the faithful. The church can be described as those who make a personal, communal response to God's action in Jesus Christ. They are those who believe, who call upon the name of our Lord Jesus Christ. "To the church of God which is at Corinth, to those sanctified in Christ Jesus, called to be saints together with all those who in every place call on the name of our Lord Jesus Christ, both their Lord and ours" (1Cor 1:2).

We are servants. The church can be described as those who adopt the servant role of Jesus Christ. Because Jesus was our servant, we are to be the servant of others. "For what we preach is not ourselves, but Jesus Christ as Lord, we your servants for Jesus' sake" (2Cor 4:5). To be a servant or a slave of Christ is to imitate his lowliness, humiliation and suffering; to be his witness; and to proclaim his gospel and kingdom. It was a common custom of New Testament authors to introduce themselves as "slaves of God," and to refer to the church as a community of slaves. "But now that you have been set free from sin and have become slaves of God, the return you get is sanctification and its end, eternal life" (Rom 6:22).

We are the people of God. The church claims to receive the covenant relationship which God established with Israel. They continue in this covenant, yet it is renewed as a "new covenant in Christ's blood." The church is called the "Israel of God" (Gal 6:16). The *Shema* is accepted by the church as addressed to them (Mk 12:29). "The people of God" include all those who live by faith in God's covenant promises from the very beginning to the last day.

We are all priests. Jesus Christ is the high priest who brings final atonement for the sins of the world through his suffering and death. Because each believer identifies with Jesus Christ, the high priest, then the church itself is considered to be a royal priesthood (1Pet 2:5, 9). The church's duty is to offer spiritual sacrifices. Believers present themselves, their bodies, as a living sacrifice (Rom 12:1). There is sharing in suffering and in ministering to corporate needs (Phil

2:17, 25, 30); they minister to others through financial aid (Rom 15:16, 27). In a similar theme, the church is the temple of God, Jesus Christ being the cornerstone (Eph 2:20-21). The church also becomes a temple through the presence of God, the Holy Spirit, and Jesus Christ. "Do you not know that you are God's temple, and that God's spirit dwells in you?" (1Cor 3:16).

We are the family of God. The church is referred to as the household, or family of God. God is the one who owns and rules the house, who dwells within it. In relation to God, the family members are dependent and obedient, and are good stewards. Some common terms used here are "sons of God" (Rom 9:26) and "children of God" (Rom 8:16). In addition, the church is spoken of as a "brotherhood" (1Pet 2:19; Mt 23:8) as well as the "bride of Christ." These images express the closeness and sense of belonging which Christians have for one another and for Christ.

We are a vineyard, a flock. By using agricultural examples, the church's dependence on God, the necessity of producing fruit, and the process of judgment, are all made clear. Christians are God's vineyard; they must stay fixed to the vine (Jesus Christ), and expect pruning in order to produce good fruit (Jn 15:1-6). Those who do not produce good fruit are "cut off." Christians are also God's flock. We must know the voice of our shepherd, watch out for the wolves (Mt 2:15) and not get "lost" (Mt 18:10-14).

We are the Body of Christ. Christians are bound together in a community of life, over which Christ is the head. All members of the body are mutually dependent, share in suffering, and are woven together through the power of love. Each person receives gifts and talents from Christ to be used for the sake of others. There are many "parts" of the body, and each of them, though different, is important. Christ, as the head of his body and the source of authority, loves, sanctifies, and saves the body.

So if we ask the question "Who are you?" to the early church, the answer is very full! The fullness grows out of Jesus Christ himself; "the Word became flesh and dwelt among us, full of grace and truth" (Jn 1:14). The church of today affirms this same identity. We can say, "I am a Christian," and this statement touches every aspect of our lives. "Who we are" concerns both the deepest parts of our hearts and our outer relationship with our whole world. But most profoundly it concerns our relationship with our very God, for "who we are" is based entirely upon the love and grace of God through Jesus Christ.

Now to the New Testament church we shall ask the question, "How are you structured?" There are some basic ideas that we can understand about the organization of the early church, although it is impossible to be specific. Our uncertainties are caused by (1) Paul's not dealing with the matter clearly, and (2) different methods being used in different areas. However, certain things can be understood.

The twelve disciples chosen by Jesus came to be the Apostles and were the undisputed authorities in the early church. An apostle was anyone who personally received a direct calling from the living or risen Christ (1Cor 9:1). Thus Paul was also an apostle, as was James, the brother of the Lord (1Cor 15:7; Gal 1:19) and probably Barnabas (1Cor 9:6). Paul considered the position of apostle to be the chief and highest gift of ministry in the church (1Cor 12:28; Eph 4:11).

The next appointment for ministry is found in Acts 6:1-6. The "Twelve" appointed seven men to "serve tables" so that the Apostles could devote themselves to prayer and the ministry of the Word. These seven include Stephen and Philip, who are also known as preachers and evangelists. Some people have tried to link the seven to the office of deacon, but there is no direct evidence for this.

The duties of elders are not described in the New Testament, though they probably had the authority which the Jewish Elders had. Elders are mentioned in the book of Acts as being part of the Jerusalem and Ephesian churches. Paul and Barnabas ordained elders for their mission churches to be the responsible leaders in the absence of the Apostles (Acts 14:23). It is not clear whether bishops and elders were the same position. However, bishops also were authoritative in the church.

I Timothy 3:8-13 describes the qualities a deacon should have. The work of the deacons was to minister to the physical needs of others through distributing offerings and acts of mercy. The inspiration of this office is Christ himself, who "came not to be served but to serve" (Mk 10:45). Paul also uses the word "deacon" to describe Timothy (I Thess 3:2), Tychicus (Col 4:7) and Epaphras (Col 1:7) who assist him in evangelizing.

Teachers and prophets were not ordained as elders and deacons were. They were chosen because of their gifts for preaching and teaching and their openness to the inspiration of the Holy Spirit. Prophets and teachers often wandered from place to place, and churches depended upon them for instruction and inspiration.

The early Christians placed a high priority on spiritual gifts, an emphasis which was more important than a Christian's office. Paul saw ministry more as an opportunity for service and grace rather than as a hierarchical position. Every member of a church had a charism of the Spirit for the edification of all. Faith, hope and love were the most important, speaking in tongues probably the least important. These gifts were to be tested for genuineness, whether they were upbuilding to others. The importance of a "charismatic" ministry is reflected in the earliest ordination prayers, from Hippolytus' *Apostolic Tradition,* which prays to God to "pour forth the power that is from Thee of the princely spirit" and to "grant the spirit of grace."

And so we find that the ecclesiastical ranks in the early church included "apostles, prophets, teachers, workers of miracles, healers, helpers, administrators, and speakers in various kinds of tongues" (ICor 12:28). By the time of Ignatius and Polycarp (120 CE) these would be structured to the offices of bishops, elders (or presbyters), and deacons.

WOMEN IN THE EARLY CHURCH

Now we turn to the question with which we are most concerned. In what way did women fit into the early church? In our first section of "who the church is," there is no question women were full participants. We can say, yes, women are justified, women are faithful, women are servants of Christ, women are among the people of God, women are priests, women are part of Jesus' flock, women are daughters of God, women are part of the body of Christ. In every aspect of "who the church is," women are definitely included. How could it be otherwise? And as full participants they are also heirs to all the promises of God in Christ: new life, freedom, grace upon grace, the power and gifts of the Spirit, and being one in Christ.

However, when we come to the positions of authority or rank within the church, we find women are not so quickly included. The "Twelve" were men; the "seven" were men. There are no female elders or bishops named. In Romans 16:2, Paul mentions Phoebe as a deaconess. Beyond the New Testament, the records of Pliny the Younger, governor of Bithynia in 112, mention that he had put to torture two Christian handmaidens who were called deaconesses. Of teachers and prophets, there are several women named. Priscilla and Aquilla are a wife-husband team who "risked their necks for my (Paul's) life" (Rom 16:3-4). Priscilla and her husband showed Apollos "the way of God more accurately," who in turn went on to convert many others (ICor 3:1-9, 21-23). The four daughters of Philip are prophetesses (Acts 21:9). Paul sends greetings to his co-worker, Junia (Rom 16:7). In addition, Paul assumes that women were prophesying in the churches, because in I Corinthians 11:5, Paul asks that women have their heads covered when prophesying. Paul's statement that women should keep silent in church (I Cor. 14:34-35) springs from a concern for "decency and order" within a local congregation, not a dictate for women of all times and places. Paul's admonition in I Timothy 2:11-15 concerns the need for women to be learners and students, in humility, before they would teach. If this passage were taken at face value, Paul would be contradicting the gospel of grace and freedom which he lived and died for.

So on the one hand, or theologically speaking, women are included one hundred percent! But practically, when it comes to authority and leadership, women are minimally involved, at least they are given very little credit. It would seem correct that women were also apostles, elders, stronger characters in the New Testament story. What conclusions can we draw? That this is the "correct" way—that men should lead and women should follow? No, I think not.

I think that the grace and freedom and strength which Jesus Christ fully lived and which he passes on to every Christian and every church are too great and full for us. Our fears, our traditions, our sins—are yet very blinding and constricting. First and foremost, every person is a sinner. We are selfish, fearful, proud. We are afraid to touch, afraid to see, afraid to act. The Gospel of Jesus Christ would sweep all these allusions and falsehoods away. Because of this great freedom Jesus was killed. He was crucified because he was too full of this grace and forgiveness. This theology of grace was also too great for the early church. The "new wine" was put into bags of tradition and sin. How could they change so quickly? How could they alter thousands of years of tradition? How could women be practically "equal"? Humankind is weak, living in darkness. And so sin is the cause of our slowness in receiving grace, both for the New Testament church and for the church of today. The early church believed that all authority and power came from God in Jesus Christ. So if Jesus held the power, what did it matter which of his flock would lead the others? If the qualification for leadership is servanthood (Mt 20:26-27), what does it matter if the servant is a man or a woman? If Jesus said that among his followers, we should not "exercise authority over one another" (Mt 20:25), then how could others object if a woman serves with teaching and preaching?

The church is tainted with the sins of the ages. Today our primary idea of power and authority comes not from the Scriptures but from our society, where money, status, and manipulation are respected. We find comfort in knowing our "place"; we do not consider one another as equals. The "curse" upon women, as found in Genesis, is still very active in society, that the man shall rule over the woman.

And so the church lives in tension, a tension between the power of sin and the call of grace. Women in particular live in this tension. Fear and pride pull a woman down; grace and strength call her forward. How should a woman act? How should a woman speak? What should a woman hope for? Let a woman's light, her path, her hope, her strength, her salvation—be Jesus Christ. Everything else is idolatry.

SUGGESTIONS FOR THE PRESBYTERIAN CHURCH IN TAIWAN

The question which now remains to be asked is: How shall we help women in Taiwan move toward fuller ministry? What can be done to support and encourage women's effort for wholeness and equality?

The answer lies in two areas: personal and public. The personal area includes each woman's faith, calling, attitude. The public area deals with church structure and programs. Both the personal and public areas are very important. Here are my suggestions for what needs to be done in the Presbyterian Church of Taiwan.

Personally, every woman should claim her rights as a daughter of God. She should know herself as forgiven, gifted, empowered, and equal—through Christ our Savior. No longer does the law of sin and subjugation bind her; sensing her worth and capabilities, she should develop her confidence so that she will not fearfully turn away from challenges or opportunities; she is free under the lordship of Christ. Every woman should develop her relationship to Christ and grow in Christ. She should show forth the fruit of the Spirit so that all honor and glory can be given to God.

Every woman needs to recognize male chauvinism where it exists. This can be a very difficult thing to do for it means changing a lifetime of responses. But until chauvinism is noted and confronted, the patterns will not change.

Every woman should learn how to express her anger, because a lifetime of being a secondary person brings deep anger and resentment. If her anger is not expressed, it cripples both herself and her relationships. However, women should recognize and express their anger in ways which are upbuilding: through sharing with a friend, confession, prayer, writing, and other ways.

Every Christian woman should enjoy being a woman. The goal is not to be a man! The goal is to be a woman, and reflect that image of God as fully as possible. Publicly, women should intentionally be placed in positions of authority within every level of church structure. Then both men and women can see that, yes, women are capable and effective.

Women's Studies/Theology should be taught at the seminaries, preferably by women. It is generally known that seminaries set the trends within the church. Because many theological students do not consider women's issues to be of any concern, there is no inclination for growth or change. Even the women students of theology are unaware of the wealth of material and ideas written on their behalf.

Women faculty members should be hired at the seminaries and Bible College in the area of Bible and theology, as well as other disciplines. Aside from providing a strong and positive role model for other women, this would assure students of the value the church places upon women. A woman faculty person could become a spokesperson for feminist issues as she perceives them.

The three Presbyterian seminaries should be consistent and fair in assigning all students to field work or church positions. In the past the women students have received little, if any, assistance from the seminary in securing positions. This must stop.

The Association for Theologically-Trained Women in Taiwan should hold more seminars and conferences. Their emphasis on education, growth, and mutual support for women church leaders is very good; but there needs to be more. They should encourage local support groups for women to be formed.

Women on all committees of the church should be encouraged to attend the meetings and to participate as fully as possible.

In conclusion, I would like to emphasize that God's calling is the most important thing. Women should become ministers and church leaders only because of God's call. Women do not become leaders or ministers in order to threaten men. We do not want to argue and fight about position and authority. But we women want to serve God fully, using all our talents and strengths. We want men to know that we are not their enemies. Our purpose is not to threaten them; it is to serve God and to work "in the Yoke" with our fellow Christians, that God may be glorified through all that we say, do and think.

4

New Ways of Being Church
I. A Catholic Perspective

Christine Tse (Hong Kong)

INTRODUCTION

When I accepted the invitation to present this paper here in Oaxtepec I was fully aware that I am not a trained theologian in the academic sense of the word. I am more qualified, perhaps, as one who is involved and concerned with developing a process of theologizing in Hong Kong and, to a certain extent, in the countries of Asia, which I frequently visit.

Since I am to speak for Asia, my first response was to interview people who are in touch with and have knowledge about women in Asian countries. My desire to begin with the experience of Asian women was greatly enhanced by the country reports presented at the Seventh Asian Meeting of Religious (AMOR VII) in Korea in 1985. These reports were given by women religious from Japan, Korea, Taiwan, Hong Kong, Thailand, Philippines, Indonesia, Sri Lanka, Bangladesh, India, and Pakistan, in consultation with religious in their own countries. So the reports can be seen as fairly representative of the views of the religious in their respective countries. In the background, there is also my involvement in EATWOT's national and Asian theological meetings.

Having said this, however, it is important to remember that religious women are but a minority of the women of Asia. They are not representative of women in Asia as a whole, except insofar as they are part of the women in the church. Religious women, in fact, have a closer working relationship to the institutional church in administering its religious institutes than to grassroots communities.

My approach is similar to a community model of theological reflection presented by a Catholic feminist theologian, Dr. Mary Hunt, whose course

I attended in New York in the summer of 1986. According to Mary Hunt, "theology emerges basically from people's sharing of their work, their faith and their lives." She defined the process of theologizing as the "organic and communal sharing of insights, stories and reflections on questions of ultimate meaning and value." This process is what the meeting of AMOR are promoting and is the basis of the reports I have been using for my own discussion here.

KINDS OF PARTICIPATION OF WOMEN IN THE CHURCH

Women have always participated in the activities of the church. Research has shown that the early Christian movement included women's leadership and could therefore be called "equalitarian." Elisabeth Fiorenza found that women played a very important role in the history of the church by participating in and influencing the spread of Christianity. She thought that Galilean women were decisive not only for the extension of the Jesus movement to Gentiles but also for the very continuation of this movement after Jesus' arrest and execution.[1]

Nowadays, the presence and coordination of a great number of women religious and committed lay women, both single and married, who are working at various levels of church activities, have become essential to the vitality of the Asian church. According to the reports presented at AMOR VII, women religious are active in pastoral work such as teaching catechism, family visits, hospital ministry, and assistance to parish groups and activities. They are respected by the laity as well as needed by the priests in the parishes. Therefore we cannot ignore their participation in, and contribution to, the church in Asia.

In the area of formal education, it is invariably true that lay women and women religious have played a leading role in running Catholic nurseries, health activities, primary and secondary schools, and colleges. Not only do sisters head these educational institutions, they also supervise and train leaders through them. These leaders become a driving force in the church. One modern criticism is that these institutions catered to the elite and didn't change their values. Did we really educate with leadership as a goal?

At the same time, relatively few reports have mentioned the involvement of women religious in justice and peace activities, which have become an important development in Asia. There may be several reasons for this: first most women religious in Asia are still not aware of justice and peace work; second, justice and peace work is done more as part-time work and does not therefore enter the mainstream of activities mentioned above; and third, justice and peace work is more comfortably done outside the church structure to avoid possible confrontation with the hierarchy or the bishop's conferences which might hurt them.

HOW DO ASIAN WOMEN SEE THEMSELVES IN THE CHURCH?

In the AMOR reports, it is commonly seen that women believe that they exert a basic, motivating power, that they are an invisible force that continually sustains the life of the Christian community. There is a marked divergence in how they feel about their participation in the church. Some are rather happy because their contribution is much valued within the church; they see this as a step forward from the dependent position that has been traditionally allocated to women. In all Asian culture, except a relatively few tribal matriarchal cultures, there is the stereotypical female who is expected to be silent, passive, and submissive in the patriarchal family and religious system.

Women do not take part in basic policy decisions; their decision-making power is limited to the practical implementation of plans. Women religious are feeling, in various degrees, that their role is secondary in a male-dominated church where the hierarchy assumes the right to decide the role of sisters in the church, their suitability for sacramental ministry, the dress they wear, and the organization of their community life. This is even more true for local religious congregations.

In several dioceses within some Asian countries trends are emerging toward greater collaboration between sisters and priests in different fields of ministry. However, some can question whether the inclusion of women in ministries is just a form of tokenism or is a real step beyond the narrow cultural and social barries, enabling the women and the priests to work as partners in a team-spirit. For example, the permission given to some lay women and women religious to distribute Holy Communion can be just a means of lessening the burden of some of the parish priests, in the absence of male religious or suitable laymen. It is not necessarily a recognition of women's worth or participation in ministerial work.

PATRIARCHY LEGITIMATES HIERARCHY

What has happened to cause and strengthen the patriarchal structure in the church today?

The origin of patriarchy in the church is believed to be related to the apologetic writings of the post-Pauline and Petrine periods which sought to limit women's leadership roles in the Christian community to merely supplementary roles. This ignored the attitude of the evangelists John and Mark, who were both seen to accord women apostolic and ministerial leadership. Susan T. Foh has a more detailed interpretation of Paul, which I am not going to elaborate here. Paul seems to contradict himself when, in Galatians 3:28, he says, "There is no such thing as Jew and Greek, slave and freeman, male and female, for you are one person in Christ," for in another of his epistles he legitimizes submission of women by adapting it to the Greco-Roman patriarchal structure.[2]

Augustine of Hippo (fourth century) promoted the idea that woman is created to help man, on the assumption that Eve's body is made from the side of Adam, even though the formation of both of their bodies flows from a divine act. In other words, the person of Eve takes her existence from the person of Adam, since she depends on him for the matter of her body. Augustine's theory on the formation of Eve from the side of Adam establishes a relation that has served as rule for the relationship of man and woman in general. For Augustine, the ideal society demanded a harmonious order established by a hierarchical relationship between a superior and an inferior, and he identified femininity with inferiority, and maleness with superiority. Thomas Aquinas reinforced this in the thirteenth century, and since then the exclusion of women in the hierarchy has been strongly rooted within the church.[3]

Up to today, despite new biblical studies and new interpretations on and about the Christian community as a discipleship of equals (equality in sharing goods did not last long—not for any theological reason but simply because of human nature), the church is still holding a very rigid position regarding the type of ministry women can exercise in the church. This is clearly seen in an exchange of letters between the Vatican and the Anglican Archbishop of Canterbury. The exchange was specifically over the right to change a tradition that has been unbroken throughout the history of the Catholic Church Universal in the East and in the West.

The Archbishop of Canterbury wrote in a letter to Cardinal Willebrands (Dec. 18, 1985) about a conviction expressed synodically by a number of provinces of the Anglican Communion that "on the Anglican side•there has been a growing conviction that there exist in Scripture and Tradition no fundamental objections to the ordination of women to the ministerial priesthood."

Willebrands's reply (June 17, 1986) leads us very much to think about the Augustinian connection. He wrote:

> We can never ignore the fact that Christ is a man. His male identity is an inherent feature of the economy of salvation, revealed in the scriptures and pondered in the Church. The ordination only of men to the priesthood has to be understood in terms of the intimate relationship between Christ the redeemer and those who, in a unique way, cooperate in Christ's redemptive work. The priest represents Christ in his saving relationship with his Body the Church. He does not primarily represent the priesthood of the whole People of God. However unworthy, the priest stands *in persona Christi.*

Of course, let us not forget that earlier Pope John Paul II had already pointed out to the Archbishop of Canterbury in a letter (Dec.20,1984) that "In those same years the increase in the number of Anglican Churches which admit, or are preparing to admit, women to priestly ordination constitutes, in the eyes of the Catholic Church, an increasing obstacle to that progress."

Interestingly enough, the studies of an internationally known psychotherapist[4] show that the very structure of most theological assumptions results in a dominance-submission scheme. In this scheme, power is at the top and total powerlessness is at the bottom.

Ann Wilson Schaef has made studies in numerous workshops conducted with women. She explored how these women see God, and humankind in relation to God; and how male and female relate to each other. The results may be tabulated thus:

GOD	HUMANKIND	MALE	FEMALE
male	childlike	intelligent	emotional
omnipotent	sinful	powerful	weak
omniscient	weak	brave	fearful
omnipresent	stupid or dumb	good	sinful
immortal	mortal	strong	like children
eternal			

These findings led to the conclusion that, in people's minds, Male is to Female what God is to Humankind. The myth of the domination of man over woman is supported by our theology to sustain a hierarchical structure. In this structure, God dominates over men; men dominate over women; women dominate over children; children dominate over animals; and animals dominate over the plants and earth.

THE ASIAN SCENE

To the surprise of our sisters in the West, what they have been saying about male domination in society and in the church is not only true of their sisters in Asia, it is even more cruel in form.

Asia has a long history of its own. This has been continuously enriched by its various and long civilizations, rich cultures and traditions, eventful historical, social, and political changes throughout the centuries. However, among the variety of differences, one common feature that emerges all through Asia is the subjugation of women to men, both at home and in society at large. Matriarchal societies were short-lived, and those rare matriarchal societies that still exist today are to be found mainly in tribal communities.

Our sisters in the West might be shocked even at the thought that some women are still being burned alive in India today for failing to satisfy their husbands with the amount of dowry demanded, that the evidence law in Pakistan (*Diyat* and *Qasas*) virtually reduces a woman to half a human being since the testimony of two women is needed to equal that of one man. *Qasas* debars women from evidence in case of murder, sexual offenses, theft, and drinking; even when the husband is murdered in the presence of his wife, her evidence has no value at all. *Diyat* (blood money) rules that when a woman is murdered, the compensation awarded the unfortunate family of the woman is half that awarded when the murdered person is a man.

Women in China or in countries whose cultures and traditions are influenced by Confucian thought are used to considering themselves virtuous if they accept everything with passivity and quiet resignation. A woman is subservient to her father before she is married, to her husband after marriage, and to her oldest son when she becomes a widow. Education is either denied to girls or given first to boys in the family.

Chinese women in the past had to endure the torturous practice of foot-binding. Muslim women have suffered the inhuman practice of circumcision so that they can never enjoy sex. In general, most women of all religions in Asia, except Christianity, have had to tolerate some form of legalized polygamy. Even today, this cruel treatment of women continues.

It is against this background that Christianity came to the East. Hence the patriarchal structure became even more deep-rooted. Furthermore, since the church is the religious minority in most of the countries in Asia, the church cannot make itself totally free from Islamic influences or Confucian traditions even if it would like to.

THE ROLE AND CONTRIBUTION OF WOMEN IN NEW WAYS OF BEING CHURCH

New ways of being church are (a) returning to the spiritual kingdom of Isaiah (11:6-9) wherein different categories of creatures are depicted as living together peacefully: the wolf and the lamb, the calf and the bear, the sucking child and the asp; (b) returning to the teaching of Paul, who wants no more division, for "you are one in Christ" (Gal 3:28); (c) returning to the teaching of Vatican II that the church is a mystery, a sacrament of union with God and of union with persons, a people related to God through Christ, an ever new responding in the spirit to the signs of the times (Constitution on the Church in the Modern World nos. 1,4); (d) returning to the 1971 Synod of Bishops' document, "Justice in the World" (chap.3), which says: "we also urge that women should have their own share of responsibility and participation in the community life of society and likewise of the church." In new ways of being church, women can make many contributions.

Conscientization

Women have to go through a process to break the mindset that induces them automatically and spontaneously to assume an inferior role to men. Paolo Freire would call this a "culture of silence." In this respect, I am fortunate to have the chance to visit many women's groups in Asia and witness how they are going through this process of conscientization and what kind of efforts they are making.

One of the signs of the times is that Asian women who have been excluded from the full dignity of the human person by Asian culture and by the patriarchal church have awakened to this harsh reality. Asian church women see the biblical and Vatican II messages cited above as a continuous call on them to experience a sense of being church in a new way. They see how the patriarchal structure obstructs the application of equal personhood and equal discipleship in the church.

Conscientization enhances women's efforts to deepen the study of the

Scriptures, their ability to name values and recognize unique contribution to church and society. As Christians, our lives are closely related to the Scripture and to how the church teaches us to live according to the Scriptures. Many Asian women are trying now to reinterpret the Scriptures and are reworking the text with inclusive language and meaning. The way we interpret things and the way we formulate our language definitely have an impact on the way we live, for this is how our consciousness and conviction are developed.

Most of us Asians have experienced how our colonizers governed us during and even after colonization. Though it was primarily a political and military rule during the period of colonization, it was through the acculturation of the middle-class intellectual to the colonizers' mentality that colonization was prolonged even after the colonizers had physically withdrawn. The medium of preservation of the status quo is often the imposition of the colonizers' language, values, and culture.

Inclusiveness as a Model or Key

Women are called to restore inclusiveness, equality, and harmony in the church. They are called to do away with control and the grabbing of power in all human relationships. They are also called not to abandon the church or surrender to apathy; they are called to be confident in the spirit, deepening their experience of the Christ within the church so that the church can be renewed.

Asian women have long suffered oppression from the patriarchal structure. They do not want to counteract this by replacing it with a matriarchal structure, which can be equally oppressive. Instead they are promoting an inclusive structure. This openness and inclusiveness is not only essential for the Asian women's movement but also a key element for the Asian people's movement to liberate themselves from oppression of all kinds. Otherwise women might just replace one dictatorship with another form of dictatorship, if they are also exclusive. Change of structures and change of mindset are consonant with the emphasis of the church on the importance of having both internal and external conversions.

Efforts to be inclusive have brought about a good ecumenical exchange between women of different faiths, first among Catholics and Protestants, then among Christian, Hindu, Buddhist, and Muslim women as well. The inclusive approach that feminist theologians propose leads women to be flexible and open. Since they do not have to defend a particular theory or methodology of their own, they can be more sensitive to the needs of others. They can learn more by listening to ideas and approaches that are different from their own. Thus they will also become more understanding and supportive.

Exclusion of women in teaching theology until recent years was partly due to the patriarchal church. Inclusion of women in teaching theology will help to shape the teaching and preaching of the church for alternative experiences within the accepted patriarchal theology. One of the implications of inclusiveness is an expanding ministry for women or the inclusion of women's priesthood. This movement is stronger within the Protestant churches in Asia. Discussions among, and demands from, the Catholic women are relatively weak. One of the reasons for this is that the Vatican is very strong in its desire to maintain an exclusive and male-dominated hierarchy. Another reason is that women religious cannot make statements on such a serious matter without the approval of their religious congregation, which is subject to Vatican scrutiny. And because many women are as traditional as men, they themselves are not changing so far, sometimes even hindering other women from changing.

The Protestant women who have been ordained as pastors have often had the negative experience of being looked upon as substitutes for men, rather than being regarded as equal and independent. In fact, it is common that the community of Christian leaders will not easily approve a woman candidate who requests to be ordained if she is intending to get married, whereas marriage is greatly favored for male pastors. Protestant women have complained that although more and more women study in schools of theology, by and large these schools adopt a discriminatory approach in education: for men, the training is mostly in preparation for ordination as ministers, but for women the focus is on how to be the pastor's wife or a lay teacher in the parish. To be inclusive is to see ministry as flowing from gifts rather than as based on gender.

Team Ministry

The recent attempts within the Catholic Church in Asia to team up both priests and women for spiritual direction (counseling, retreat work, etc.) have produced new and very positive experiences. Traditionally, spiritual direction is an exclusive right of the male clergy, which, according to some feminist theologians, can be used as a means to control women and the laity in order to maintain the superiority of the celibate male clergy in the church.

So far, this kind of team spiritual direction has been well received in Asia. Priests who are working as co-partners on the team or priests who favor such spiritual direction have remarked with enthusiasm about how they have been enriched by the cooperation of women. Priests have appreciated women's capacity to enhance a warm and loving human relationship, and their ability to relate to a God who is personal and human as opposed to an abstract God. In fact, members of the church—even males—are now beginning seriously to question the patriarchal system and its negative effects on them. They recognize that women can help to restore such values as friendship and intimacy to the church. These values have been largely discouraged by the church culture throughout history, but they are values that modern psychologists confirm as essential to human existence.

In the same way, women can play roles in the parish team and other arenas for action. Women can contribute in curriculum development. They can help write and select the texts for catechetics and schools, pointing out how sex-stereotyping of male-female roles is fostered in the texts and pictures.

Action for Justice

As one who has been involved full-time in justice and peace work for a number of years in Asia, I have the conviction that this is an area where women must open their eyes to discover new ways of being church.

Action for justice has been termed a constitutive dimension of preaching the gospel by the Synod of Bishops' document "Justice in the World." Asian women's experiences allow them to see the effects of working for justice, a concern that the Asian churches have gradually incorporated into their pastoral works.

Through actual exposures to Asia's realities, through training, analysis, and reflection, Asian people begin to see more easily why they are poor and oppressed. They also see why Asia is kept poor and underdeveloped, why militarism has such a strong hold in their countries, and why there is such a violation of human rights. Theological reflections urge Asian people to come up with a Christian response toward this situation.

Asian women are "holding up half of the sky." If they are moved to action arising from this consciousness, Asian societies are bound to change in a positive direction. And women have the power to change societies if they introduce the concept of justice wherever they are present. Women are the frequent churchgoers; they are seen more frequently attending church activities and activities related to their own community of slums, villages, housing estates, and so on; they are the ones taking care of the children at home. Therefore their influence in these areas can be very substantial and penetrating if they have a conviction that things can be changed for the better and if they work toward it.

I would like to emphasize here that women from all walks of life, all levels of intelligence, and differing experience can contribute equally, though in different ways, to the same goal. Some studies on the level of political involvement of women in Hong Kong show that housewives who are living in the crowded, low-cost government-housing estates are frequently and actively involved in matters concerning their community. Their actions are very political on a local level. On the other hand, middle-class intellectual women are not so actively involved in local or community politics, as their common felt needs are not so great. They can live more or less independently in private houses, although sometimes they are geared to politics on the macro level.

Due to the cultural and religious background, and due to Asia's semifeudal system, Asian people and especially women are generally apathetic toward anything political. However, Asian women are now getting involved in political actions that will improve their lives. This is a trend that will grow and will have far-reaching consequences. Asians are beginning to realize that to do nothing is to give their silent consent to the oppressors to continue doing harm to them.

Women can change the Asian church and the society along with it if they work to bring justice and peace education to their families. Asian children are too long under the patriarchal tutelage. They will grow up dominating others as they have learned from their "fathers" the patriarchy, and they will accept domination without challenging it. If Asian women gain social consciousness, they can help to create the same process in the family, in the community, and in the church, where members are invited to express their views freely, to share their problems and find the solutions together. This process demands creative criticism, openness, inclusiveness, acceptance, and democracy—and these are what our church and society need today.

DEMYTHOLOGIZING THE PATRIARCHAL STRUCTURE

The fate of Asian women today reflects the impact of the patriarchal structure, which many Asian female theologians have identified. Within this patriarchal structure, all the positions in the hierarchy (popes, bishops, priests, deacons) are occupied exclusively by a minority of celibate males who either are not aware of women's life and experience or are not open to face the need of change in the patriarchal structure, or both.

Biblical scholars and theologians are questioning whether the patriarchal structure of church and the antiwoman attitude were intended by Jesus when he began to preach and establish the kingdom on earth, or whether these developments are only historically conditioned. In Mark 10:29-30, commenting on Jesus' answer to Peter's question, "Who then can be saved?" Elisabeth Fiorenza says that, in the answer of Jesus, "fathers" are among those to be left behind; "fathers" are not included in the new kinship to which the disciples aspire. For Fiorenza and for many Asian women, this is an implicit rejection of the power and status of the "fathers" and all patriarchal structures in the messianic community. Therefore this rejection gives rise to what Fiorenza terms "the discipleship of equals."[5]

In Mark 3:33-35 Jesus proposes the new structure for the messianic community. In this community, the old way of relationships of "mothers," "brothers," and so forth is to be replaced by a new principle, that of doing the will of God. Christ wants us to be free and to enjoy the freedom of being children of God; we need to take Christ's words seriously.

In principle, as Christians we all believe in the resurrection of Christ, because it is an important proof that Christ is divine. If so, we should also believe that "when the dead rise to life, they will be like the angels in heaven" (Mt 22:30). In other words, the Christ who rose from the dead is no longer conditioned by sex, race, or nationality. Christ becomes all for all. Everyone in the messianic community becomes a disciple among equals.

Logically therefore, it is no wonder that feminist theologians call it a great scandal to see that, beginning with the early church and continuing to the church of today, the institutional church has not obeyed the command of Jesus to "call no one father." Asian women are just beginning to get involved in reinterpreting the Bible to find its deepest salvific and liberating significance for humanity as a whole. One important step is to demythologize the existing patriarchal structure with all its implications.

NOTES

1. Elisabeth Schussler Fiorenza, *In Memory of Her* (New York: Crossroad Publishing Co., 1983).

2. Susan T. Foh, *Women and the Word of God, a Response to Biblical Feminism,* (Presbyterian and Reformed Publishing Co., 1979).

3. Kari Elisabeth Borresen, *Subordination and Equivalence: The Nature and Role of Women in St. Augustine and Aquinas* (Lanham, Md.: University Press of America, 1981).

4. Ann Wilson Schaef, *Women's Reality: An Emerging Female System in the White Male Society* (Minneapolis: Winston Press, 1985).

5. Elisabeth Schussler Fiorenza, *In Memory of Her.*

II. A Protestant Perspective

Yong Ting Jin (Malaysia)

THEOLOGICAL REFLECTIONS ON WOMEN IN THE CHURCH

At the Asian Women's Consultation on Total Liberation from the Perspective of Asian Women, held in Manila (Nov. 21-30, 1985), varied expressions were given to reflect theologically on women in society and church in particular, as found in the statement below:

> Oppression of women is SINFUL. This systemic sin is rooted in organized and established economic, political, and cultural structures with PATRIARCHY as an overarching and all-pervading reality that oppresses women.

As church people, we have come to realize that the highly patriarchal churches have definitely contributed to the subjugation and marginalization of women. Thus we see an urgent need to reexamine our church structure, traditions, and practices in order to remedy injustices and to correct misinterpretations and distortions that have crippled us.[1]

Such is the existing reality of the church! Apparently the church has become an institution, with all its goods, services, laws, doctrines, liturgies, rites, ministries, structures, and traditions. The entire mechanism developed gradually, resulting in a pyramidal hierarchy. This form of domination is typical of the patriarchal system, pervading all spheres of life. Particularly in the arena of church politics, the power game ranks high, breeding corruption, cultivating and securing superiority, exhibiting abuses of power for political motives and vested interests. Yet this is the leadership model we are given to follow. The image and marks of the church as *ecclesia* are scarred.

Leonardo Boff[2] made a most provocative critique of the Roman Catholic Church and the ways in which power, sacred power, is manipulated and abused. This is in no way any less true of the Protestant Church. His contention was that since the fourth century the church has become prey to the forces, the dynamics of power, which have nothing to do with the power of the gospel. Again, this historical reality is confirmed repeatedly in our experiences of the institutional church today.

These are the old ways of being church—full of distortions, plagued by corruption and high-powered lip service and glaringly unjust practices. Even the so-called renewed community of the supposedly progressive ecumenical movement of men and women is not spared from this critique, as long as we too fall prey to tendencies and practices of the "old"!

The church has lost its real essence, meaning, and effects. Though there have been serious attempts and prolific theological reflections/writings to redefine the meaning of *ecclesia,* it remains an important priority for us to return yet again to an understanding of the church as *ecclesia* and faith community.

While confirming the effects of the present realities of the church and the hurts upon our lives and those of other women, the participants at the Manila Consultation experienced yet again the liberating gospel and spirit of Christ. By Jesus' breakthroughs with a tradition that would diminish one-half of humanity, we felt affirmed and empowered to presevere in our painful struggle for full humanity. Jesus demonstrated this full humanity by his own life; and the teaching of God's kingdom was one with his deeds.

In the light of the gospel truth, Jesus is GOOD NEWS to all women! We have every reason to rejoice, to be helpful, and to order our lives after the model of the new creation in Jesus Christ.

WOMEN AND NEW WAYS OF BEING CHURCH

The original Greek meaning of *ekklesia* (a gathering church) refers to a gathering of people belonging to a community. It has a common history founded on an event and the sharing of a common experience. In a theological sense, the *ekklesia* history began when a few women acted together by paying respect to their dead friend Jesus at the tomb on the Sabbath day, during which they were forbidden to do any work. Already they were doing something "new" and profound, though it was treated as an insignificant, small job! And later, as enlightened first witnesses to the (cross-) resurrection-event and a new personal experience of Jesus the risen Christ, their "storytelling" of the Good News was ridiculed and passed over as unsound. Yet this was how the *ecclesia* emerged. It was a new birth with a new identity.

Swept by the unique experience of the Spirit and its charisms at the Pentecost, the faithful believers of men and women were moved to assemble in one place, celebrating and sharing their resources and life in common. Daily they deepened their faith by examining the Scriptures and breaking bread. Care, love, and concern for one another prevailed and increased in the community— a distinctive *koinonia* indeed. The Spirit led and shaped the faith community. It bore a new, distinguishing mark and vision patterned after the life and mission of Jesus. In building up a community, the believers grew in character, individually and corporately—one and all responding to and professing the power of the gospel in the living out of their life together.

We can find, as conceived in the New Testament writings, a host of theological thinking, terms, and expressions used and described to put new meaning and content into this gathering of faithful women and men. Looking at the epistles of Peter and Paul, the *ecclesia* is characterized as the "people of God," the "body of Christ."

In fact, the term "people of God" has its deep historical roots tracing back to Old Testament times. Related to its cultural and sociological terms, the "people of God" also refers to a chosen race, a royal priesthood, a holy nation. In 1 Peter 2:5-10, they are a community called to proclaim God's saving act for all humanity.

Paul described *ecclesia* with reference to the "body of Christ" as a corporate unit. A plurality of gifts is evidenced by the members of the body. Each person has a unique and creative role to play as inspired and sustained by the Spirit. Everyone is charismatic, no one is useless. As such, each member has a decisive place in the community, but all serving one another, all having and enjoying equal dignity. There is no room for any part of the body to despise, oppress, or dominate the other: "The eye cannot say to the hand, 'I do not need you,' nor can the head say to the feet, 'I do not need you'" (1Cor.12:21). All charisms that God bestows upon each person, man and woman, young and old, must be used and shared in service and humility to the whole community.

Going back to the gospel accounts, one finds that the nature and character of *ecclesia* was initially enacted in Jesus' ministry. The great following of the "Jesus community" was a dynamic presence in the midst of the sociocultural and political setting of Palestine in the time of Jesus. However, the birth of this "Jesus community" came into being when Jesus announced the Good News of God's kingdom (*baseleia*) as the new creation. Precisely in this context the *ecclesia*, or the then "Jesus community," was understood to be a visible and dynamic sign of the kingdom vision directed toward a holistic transformation of society. This was the radical new way of being church in the widest ecumenical sense of the word.

When Jesus sought to communicate a vision of the new era, his core message was leveled against the social, cultural, political, and economic situation of the time. In favor of bringing about a total liberation to each human person and to society as a new way of life as well as a new order of society, Jesus spoke in parables. They depict pictures and scenes of life in a community where old and new values are contrasted. The story of the banquet portrays a scene of the sharing community, where an invitation is extended to people from the streets and lanes—poor, blind, and lame—until the house is full! In Jesus' understanding, a sharing community does not seek to establish its own exclusive social class, as the Pharisees were doing, separate from those we regard as inferior or subordinate. On the contrary, it seeks for inclusiveness as a definite value and way of life, doing away with social division and all forms of discrimination.

The story of the meal and how people rush for positions of honor and power, is also far from the way of life in a community. Instead, humility—a lifestyle of servanthood and self-denial, or self-emptying—is needed. Jesus taught that all power and authority must be exercised in deepest humility for the love and service of others. This is something that demands a transcendence of old attitudes and mentality; indeed, a very costly new way to discipleship!

Baseleia is good news for women! Women were the most oppressed and powerless of all, but Jesus associated with them and restored the dignity due them regardless of their social status or stigma. He affirmed the full personhood of women as being created in God's image, a concept that culture and traditions may distort and so cause women to be seen as less than human. Unlike the rabbinic tradition, Jesus taught women openly. Women were among the band of disciples following Jesus because he included women in his teaching and practice of God's kingdom. In historical reality, as the Gospels have it, women were in fact the first in faith, in terms of both their coming to faith and their quality of faith. When Jesus appeared and reached out to them at the tomb, he sent them to carry the Good News of his resurrection to the other disciples. Thus women must today rediscover their original and distinctive role in the Gospel. Precisely because of the primacy of women's faith, women played a decisive role in disclosing God's liberation history, as recounted in Matthew's and Luke's Gospels in the birth stories of Jesus.

Women were active participants in all areas of the life and mission of the early Christian communities. They were apostles, teachers, prophetesses, providers, workers, preachers, each according to her potential and God-given talents. Indeed, they were full-time partners alongside men in the Gospel of Christ.

Today, women must become fully aware and take confidence in Christ to rediscover their original and distinctive role in the Gospel. In realizing their potential they ought to reclaim their rightful place in the kingdom and God's new creation through Jesus Christ. They must receive with faith the salvation of God by grace and begin to experience anew the power of the Gospel, which sets free every person from all forms of bondage and oppression. With this faith and hope, women can, with new minds, assume in new ways the role of leaders, decision-makers, pastors, educators, teachers, prophetesses, peace-makers, theologians, and so forth. Women in the new creation must set aflame their lives and be followed in the order of faith.

The new ways of being church are modeled and implied, based on the values, characteristics, and qualities of the new as embodied in the person, life, and value system of Jesus. Every person, female and male, is summoned to participate in the building processes of the new. When the new era comes, it cannot leave the old structures and lifestyles intact. The new wine will burst the old wineskins, calling for a new creation (Mk 2:21-22). Likewise, a piece of new cloth does not match the old one. Behold, the old is passing away, and the new has come!

IMPLICATIONS OF THE WOMAN'S ROLE AND CONTRIBUTION IN THE NEW CREATION

In the light of the new-woman consciousness and of women reclaiming power in their significant role, they are empowered to play a creative role and to make positive contributions in new ways of being church. A host of things come to mind calling for a reconstruction of the old and an innovative creation of the new. The challenge is waged at all levels and dimensions of life. It goes further than the verbal, analytical perspective by expanding frontiers of action as well as involving a fuller integration of both personal and corporate lives together in a human community of women and men.

A New Lifestyle

Being a new woman in the new creation, she has to participate in the new, making it relevant by living out a lifestyle that is Christ-like. Right at the start, when Jesus announced and summoned people to the kingdom and its vision, he called for repentance. Living out the life of the kingdom, therefore, requires continuous repentance and faith in the Good News. It calls for a total change of heart, mind, and spirit—at the personal level as well as at the social, in the structures of the heart no less than in the structures of economics, politics, culture, and all other spheres of life and systems of society. Repentance is required of any new person in Christ, without bias or distinction of race, sex, and class. Here the process of repentance causes one to seek first God's *baseleia* and righteousness. Without constant repentance and search on the personal and the corporate levels, a total transformation of society will not be realized. Therefore, women too need to enter into the process of repentance and search in order to remain responsible agents in the building of a new faith community or church. While submitting herself to the spirit of God in this process, the woman must see herself playing the role of educator and preacher promoting new ways of being church as envisioned by Jesus. This is primary, prior to any concrete action, role and contribution.

An Ecumenical Role

The woman's role and contribution in new ways of being church must be approached in the widest ecumenical sense, taking into account the realities of social and religious institutions such as the church, home, and society at large. Today, increasingly, women in the church are addressing themselves to the twin tasks of total transformation in the church and in the society.

A New Exercise of Power

In the institutional church, women are faced with confronting and challenging patriarchal structures and traditions. Alternative models are needed to shape and build up a new faith community of women and men. New meanings and definitions of the leadership, power, and authority concepts must be given. In the biblical sense, Jesus speaks of being a leader and handling power in the most unworldly manner. Jesus rejected and opposed strongly the kind of power, position, status quo, and glory offered by Satan in the story of the three temptations. As a leader, Jesus washed the feet of his friends. This power is the blessing for one to live in love, in peace with justice, in community. This power is never violent or destructive, ego-centered or domineering. This power is understood, motivated, and exercised by one's set of values as patterned after the vision of God's new creation. It serves to foster, enhance, and nurture all of life. This power is dynamic and constructive because it has to do with caring, inclusiveness, peace with justice as against racism, sexism, classism, and militarism.

Today, women having past and present experiences of powerlessness may treat this as a special calling to sing of power in a new key. They are capable of exploring ways to move beyond powerlessness into new vision and meanings of power.

The new exercise of power goes with a new approach to leadership. The old model is hierarchical, bureaucratic, and exclusive. It is also based on a one-man heroic show highly motivated by a spirit of competition and a male-macho image. To be followed in the order of faith, women have to show themselves as leaders different from the male style. In Jesus' words, to be a leader, one must be a servant—a suffering servant. Women are presently practicing and sharing collective leadership. This proves a better alternative as they adopt a creative and cooperative process of decision-making, of mutuality and trust based on consensus.

A New Theological Reflection

In the present total life and mission of the church, women have a vital role to play. They are the renewing force. A primary task may be creating an educational program on a rereading of the Bible from the women's perspective. Thus women's contribution to doing theology from their lived experiences in a relevant context is crucial in the order of faith. This too leads to the formulation of worship, its content and form of liturgies; the use of language and new symbols that are inclusive of all people without distinction of gender, race, and class.

While reaching out to women in the church, some kind of creative and regular dialogue is needed between women and men, and among women themselves. This helps to build up and nurture a new community of women and men who are already engaged in the struggle for total human liberation, including the women's struggle against oppression.

Among women theologians and women making theological reflection, the need for a partnership of women and men in contributing to the total life and mission of the church is becoming more recognized. This contribution is essential, particularly in terms of maximizing women's participation in all areas and sharing in all forms of ministries, theological dialogue, and education toward partnership.

The New Faith Community

In the broadest ecumenical view, new ways of being church extends to and embraces all of creation and humanity in the whole inhabited world. The church as a faith and human community is located in the midst of the current global realities. Perhaps women find that their role is more than double as they assume the task of analyzing the situation at all levels—global, regional, and local—by translating the Good News of God's kingdom relevant to the social realities. Women become the prophetic voice as they pose challenges to other women and men to repent and live the new order of life.

The woman's role and contribution goes further than merely engaging at the level of social analysis. In the light of the greater human struggle for total liberation and social transformation, more women are moving to the forefront in the people's movement, in the peace movement, and also in consolidating their own movement.

Women in the new faith community can play a part in enabling other women to participate in women's movements around the world. Concrete concerns of the women's situation in the national or local context should be brought to the attention and care of the faith community. This is an important area of contribution by women for and with other women who are among the poorest and most oppressed of all. It can become a new missionary venture, an evangelization on new frontiers. Women in the faith community then can take a leading role in interpreting the church's mission to women who are oppressed in all sectors of the society. Issues, problems, and concerns may vary from country to country in Asia. However, these may be classified under the following broad categories:

> militarization and nuclearization, and their effects on women;
> prostitution and exploitation of women's bodies;
> exploitation of women workers;
> customs, traditions, and religious practices oppressive to women;
> racism and racial minorities;
> women in politics and people's struggles.

Concerted actions will have to be taken in response to the conditions of women listed above. Women in the church can enter into a joint endeavor with women's organizations already existing in their locality that are working with women of various sectors for consciousness-raising and toward mobilization for changes.

A New Pattern of Relationship

The home-and-family tends to be a forgotten place even though it is a basic institution of education within the larger society. However, it is a place where patriarchal attitudes, ideas and values are reinforced daily in all aspects of family life. Children grow up with stereotyped roles defined for their lives as male and female. The pattern of relationship between man and woman, husband and wife is one of a superior and a subordinate, as perpetuated and accepted by social and cultural conditionings. The home, being a most basic social and educational institution, must be transformed. The woman's role and contribution in new ways of being church should also consider educating the young, especially in the formation of minds and hearts, inculcating new values following the vision of the new order where equality, love, justice, and peace will reign.

The need for creating a new form and pattern of relationship between man and woman, husband and wife must be approached on a more personal level. It may be seen as unimportant, but in order to be fully integrated in the new, the old model and pattern of relationship must also go. New ones must be created. Women together with men will have to break through traditions and cultural practices that keep them in their respective gender roles. This involves a long and painful process. Women will have to help themselves, first of all, to break out of the roles defined for them, the image and the position that restrict them from creativity and freedom. By working through this at the personal level, half the job is already done when men and women enter consciously into an equal and mutual partnership in the total life and mission of the church.

CONCLUSION

Women, church, and new ways of being church are viewed in the perspective of God's kingdom and the new creation. It is in the light of this perspective that the woman's role and contribution are discussed. However, it is felt that this is a limited discussion. Nevertheless, the task is very demanding of all of us at all levels of change.

In obedience to our faith, let us in solidarity struggle together as members of the people of God, the body of Christ, new citizens of the kingdom, new creation made in God's image toward the vision of the New Heaven and New Earth where God's spirit, justice, peace, and love will reign and prevail in the order of life.

NOTES

1. Quoted from the statement "Asian Church Women Speak," drafted at the EAT-WOT Manila Consultation ,Nov. 21-30, 1985. See chap.11, below, page 120.

2. Leonardo Boff, *Church: Charism and Power* (New York: Crossroad Publishing Co., 1985).

5

Woman and the Holy Spirit: From an Indian Perspective

Crescy John (India)

An attempt to write anything on the Holy Spirit is comparable to finding a path on the sea. Like the ocean, the power and influence of the Holy Spirit is overwhelming, yet vague and indefinable. However, there are some spiritual compasses by which we can in some small measure identify the workings or the action of the Spirit, who has been promised to us till the end of time.

The ones that I have used in this paper are Scriptures and discernment of the action of the Spirit in the lives of Asian women, past and present, with a hesitant groping towards the future. My hope is that this effort will bring out the theological perspective that will help us to achieve the objective of this Asian Women's Consultation, which is to articulate our faith reflections on our reality in the process of total liberation.

THE HOLY SPIRIT—A MYSTERY

The Holy Spirit is a mystery in the deepest sense of the word because it transcends all our ideas and concepts. No theology or church can have the Spirit at its disposal because it "blows where it wills" (Jn 3:8). "How small a whisper do we hear?" (Job 26:13ff).

The Old Testament writers speak of experiencing the Spirit as holy (Ps 51:11; Is 63:10), as urging people to prophesy (1Sam 19:19-24; 1Kg 22.), as leading people to wise political decision (Gen 41:38; Jg 3:10; 6:34) and as imparting understanding and craftsmanship (Ex 31:3; 35:31). Israel's most profound experience of the Holy Spirit, however, was as the "strong east wind that dried up the sea" (Ex 14:21; 15:8-10), a liberative and creative experience. Also, Genesis 1 speaks of creation as the work of the Spirit of God, and again, after the crushing exilic experience, Israel longed for the new creation when

God's Spirit will be in control (Hos 13:15; Is 32:15-18).

Though scarce, the New Testament references to the Spirit are notable. Jesus did not speak of a pneumatology, but he lived in the Spirit as God's son. The "creator spirit" is at work in his birth (Lk 1:35), and it is mentioned that he "would baptize with the Spirit" (Mk 1:8). At the last passover meal, the strongest promise that he held out is that of the Paraclete as the strengthening and continuing force of God's presence in the Church.

From Mystery to Reality

For our purposes here, we do not intend to go deeper into the mystery of the Holy Spirit which would be an exercise in futility, but to review and analyse the functional or the operative aspect of the Holy Spirit, especially as it touches on the lives of Asian women, regardless of their religious tradition.

I wish therefore to take off from four scriptural bases which hopefully will throw some light on the subject from a theological standpoint.

1. The Holy Spirit will come upon you and the power of the Most High will overshadow you (Lk 1:35). This is perhaps one of the most powerful references to the Holy Spirit in the Gospels whereby a simple village maiden is empowered to be the mother of Jesus. Luke tells us of the beautiful after effects of this empowerment. Mary rose and went to the hill country to visit her cousin Elizabeth who likewise was a recipient of a powerful grace, that is, to bear a child in her old age. Mary's Magnificat is a breaking into song and stating in no uncertain terms the marvels that the Almighty had done for her.

With this as the backdrop, we can take a look at history, at the women in Christianity as well as in the other oriental religions. They can be classified into the empowered women and the depowered women. The empowering and depowering of women have taken place not only in the strictly religious sphere, but also in society, culture, tradition, laws, etc., although it would not be incorrect to say that religion has been the conditioner and the legitimizing factor behind all this.

Our Judeo-Christian Scripture offers several examples of empowered women. As we are more familiar with our Scripture we need mention here only a few of these women. One of them is Deborah, a prophetess, judge and deliverer of Israel. Her strength and abilities were so great that she could advise the generals of the army on strategic military action. She offered to go with them when Barak the general begged her to. (cf Jg 4) Judith was another brave woman who saved her people with the use of her wisdom and beauty to destroy the leader of the enemy, Holofernes. (cf Bk of Judith) Miriam, another prophetess led the women of Israel in a song of victory after the Exodus (Ex 15:20). Esther was a fine model of a caring and courageous queen who was not afraid to plead for her people before the king. (cf Bk of Esther) The woman who anointed Jesus performed a prophetic action

53

which Jesus affirmed would be told in memory of her wherever the Gospel was preached (Mk 14:3).

In the later history of the Church we have women like Catherine of Sienna who had the courage to counsel a pope to return to Rome from Avignon. Hildegard of Bingen, whose name is not so often heard, was a mystic and spiritual writer. Her poetry and other writings are of a deep and profound nature. Simone Weil was another mystic who combined radicalism with her deep spiritual insights.

In the Indian traditions and those of neighbouring countries, we have some fine examples of empowered women. Mira Bai is perhaps the most well known of the Hindu mystics of the Bhakti tradition. A devotee of the god Krishna, she incurred the wrath of her husband and family as she was totally absorbed in her spiritual pursuit. She was tried and ordered to drink a cup of poison as a death penalty, which she did fearlessly, but it is said that the poison did not work on her.

Panditha Ramabai was another extraordinary woman — a scholar, activist and reformer. Her greatness lay in the fact that she broke the sacred traditions of the Brahmins and became a Panditha (scholar) in Hindu Scriptures, which otherwise was denied to Indian women. Her life was spent in bringing about social reforms for child widows and other disadvantaged women of the Hindu tradition. She later embraced Christianity and translated the entire Bible into Marathi, one of the Indian languages.

Ancient history records that in the very early days there were women who were well-versed in the Scriptures and philosophy of the time. Ghosha was one of the oldest of such women called Brahmavadinis who were women seers and voiced Vedic wisdom through hymns. She was an outstanding woman who combined spiritual and philosophical wisdom in her writings. Her songs of wisdom have been recorded in the tenth book of the Rig Veda, one of the ancient sacred books of the Hindus.

Gargi, the daughter of a great sage, was a philosopher of repute. She had her education in the gurukulas which were forest schools akin to the ashrams. During this period known as the Vedic age, women had full opportunities for education and knowledge. It is said that she participated in a philosophical congress and could hold her own against other men philosophers of stature like the famous Yajna Valkya.

Sangamitra was the daughter of the Emperor Asoka. At this time, Buddhism was flourishing and spreading in India and Buddhist missionaries were going to neighbouring lands. Sangamitra, who was married and had a son, renounced the world and travelled to Sir Lanka to spread Buddha's teachings there.

Not only in the spiritual but also in the political sphere did Indian women make their mark. Prabhavathi Gupta stands out as a woman of great political **strength. A daughter of Chandra Gupta, she was married to another king,** Rudrasena, who died early in life. Her son was still a minor, so for thirteen years or more, she successfully ruled the kingdom as a regent.

During the Muslim period in India in the thirteenth century, we have the famous Raziyya Sultana of whom legends of gallantry are handed down to this day. She was the ruler of her country. She loved her people and ruled them wisely. She engaged in battles, riding along with her soldiers to the front, till finally she died fighting.

Besides the noteworthy women themselves, there are in the Indian tradition some concepts of empowerment like Stree Shakti and Swayamvaram which are being revived today to empower women. Stree Shakti, meaning woman power or strength, has its genesis in Saraswati, the goddess of learning from whom the Sanskrit language is supposed to have originated. In the philosophical thinking that evolved from this, the feminine concept of Shakti was considered the creative force in the universe. The women's movement, particularly of Gandhian women, is taking up this idea for the human promotion of women in the areas of justice, learning and equality.

Swayamvaram is a marriage ritual in which the bride is allowed to choose her own life partner. It is said that this was the form that existed in the very early days of history as it is mentioned in the Vedas. Among the educated and liberated women, this idea of choosing one's own husband is replacing the traditional arranged marriages, thus eliminating the problem of dowry and other miseries that go with it.

Throughout history, however, the depowerment of women has been far more pronounced than their empowerment. All subjugation and subordination of women started from the time of Eve in the creation story of the Bible. In the "fall," it was also the woman who was most affected.

The Old Testament abounds with stories of depowered women, depicted as low in status or as servile possessions of men and denied of equal rights of inheritance or power. One incident that is often unnoticed in the Bible is that of Queen Vashti who refused to parade her beauty in front of drunken men and was therefore stripped of her position and power as queen (Est 1:9).

In the early Christian era, even though there was a strong movement for a discipleship of equals, tenets for the depowerment of women soon crept in into the various churches. The injunction of Paul in his letters to the church at Corinth for women to be silent in the congregation and to be submissive to their husbands became some of the strongest legitimation for keeping women under control and subjugated.

The torture and burning of witches is a most striking example of depowerment of women. The word 'witch', Margaret Murray points out, is allied with 'wit', basically meaning 'to know'. A witch is one who 'foretells'. When this happens in the name of one of the established religions, it is called prophecy; if outside it, witchcraft. Even today in India, there are stray incidents of women being burned for witchcraft, though no such incidents are reported about men.

In the oriental or Eastern tradition, the Code of Manu from the post-Vedic era is one of the principal instruments for depowerment of women as it is still being faithfully followed today. Women become the property of men and thus lose their identity, position and power as persons in their own right.

One of the unusual patterns of depowerment of women in India is the custom of Sati. As practiced, a widow was supposed to end her life by jumping into the funeral pyre of her husband. It had a religious and economic significance. A woman's salvation was closely linked with that of her marital and maternal status. Besides, widow remarriage being unheard-of in those days, a widow was a liability to the community. Unfortunately, this age-old custom of Sati is again raising its ugly head in India.

In the Ramayana, also known as the Lakshman Rehka, the ideal wife of Rama is left in her forest hut when Rama goes hunting. It is said that Lakshmana, Rama's brother, drew a circle and asked her not to step beyond it. She did go beyond it and tragedy befell her; she was abducted by Ravana. Ironically enough, it seems that the circle of Sita, far from being a protecting factor, was a limiting one, indicative of women being confined to their own homes in today's reality. Overstepping the limits of the circle brought all the trouble. Either way, the depowering of women is indicated, whether within the circle or outside it.

The dowry system has unfortunately brought on immense agony and suffering to women. Huge dowries have been the undoing of women and their families, resulting in tragic deaths, abortion of female fetuses after amniocentic tests, and many other untold miseries.

The Christian Succession laws and the Muslim Shariat have also been cited as examples of depowerment of women. Succession laws were part of the personal law arising out of customary practice in each community. In two of the old princely states of India, namely Travancore and Cochin, acts called Succession laws were passed in the early part of this century regarding succession to property. According to these acts, the father or the head of the house is the sole owner of the family property and has the power to dispose of it as he pleases. If he dies intestate, then a daughter's share of the divided property is a mere one-fourth (one-third for Cochin) of the son's share, or 5000 rupees — whichever is less. These acts, being so discriminatory towards women, were challenged by a lady, Mrs. Mary Roy, and were nullified by the Supreme Court of India three years ago.

The Shariat or Muslim personal law is also extremely unjust to the woman, especially in its divorce formula of *talaq,* whereby a wife can be divorced very easily by a man. The case of Shah Bano, a Muslim woman of India who challenged her husband for this injustice and demanded redress, has gone down in history. The battle however is still not won as there are so many more Muslim women who are depowered and discriminated against by these unjust laws.

2. Do you know that your body is the temple of the Holy Spirit? (ICor 6:19). Paul, in his two letters to the Corinthians, repeatedly talks of the body as a temple of the Holy Spirit. A temple denotes a holy place wherein the Spirit of God dwells. Hence, it has a certain sanctity or dignity attached to it because it is the dwelling place of the Spirit.

In the Asian reality, and for that matter all over the world, the person of women has been desacralized as a sex object. It has been reduced to a symbol of 'flesh' and not 'spirit', to cater to the lustful and carnal needs of men.

Prostitution is one of the worst forms of exploitation and degradation of women. With the expansion of trade and tourism, the neo-colonial tools of exploitation, prostitution has become "the largest spin-off occupation often left politely unmentioned."[1] Today, the multinational influx is depriving women of their dignity and sacredness as persons, not to mention their share of just wages.

In India, prostitution has become a cross-cultural phenomenon, even defying caste barriers which otherwise are so rigidly maintained. One of the unique types of prostitution prevalent in India today is the Devadasi system of temple prostitution. This practice originated when Hindu kings thought that the gods should be also served by *dasis* (women who serve); hence, *deva-* (god)-*dasis*. In the beginning, these women lived a pure and devout life as they were offered to God. Later however, the practice deteriorated to prostitution as these women were forced to cater to the lust of the temple authorities who owned the places. Today, it has degenerated into a form of goddess worship and young girls are offered to the Goddess Yellamma and initiated into prostitution. A great majority of the prostitutes in Bombay are *devadasis*. Of late, there have been serious efforts to rehabilitate them and their children.

The unspeakable atrocity of female circumcision or genital mutilation is practised among the Behri Muslims of India. This is a cruel form of mutilation which goes against nature and all that the Creator endowed women for her creative function. Muslim women are becoming aware of this atrocity and some remedial measures are being taken.

Rape and violence are some of the worst kinds of indignities that can be inflicted on women. Though punishable by law, the culprits are hardly ever brought to book as the guardians of the law, the police and the judiciary, are mostly male. However, some recent cases that have been favorably judged have made headlines in the papers and women's voices are raised in protest when no action is taken. An excellent organization exists in India called the Forum against oppression of women. It was started after several rape cases were reported and the courts failed to give a correct judgment. It later tackled other cases of violence against women as well. It organizes strong action against the culprits that commit rape or any other atrocity against women and is a strong force to be reckoned with today.

The media exploitation of women is one of the subtle ways in which the person of woman is degraded under the glaze and tinsel of publicity. Films and advertisements have wreaked immense damage on women. This kind of publicity spawns a feeling of wanting to be attractive and alluring on the part of unwary women, certainly not for their own self-esteem or worth, but for the sake of being appealing to men. An exercise in comparing and contrasting men and women in ads and films will prove the point. Women's faces and bodies add glamour to an advertisement and boost the sales of the commodity, but the vast majority of them neither see nor can afford such items.

Language has also been successfully adapted to use women for sexual purposes. Examples are 'sex-appeal', 'curvaceous', 'come-hither look', words which are never used for men, but which play up the sexuality of women. Verbal hygiene is called for in the use of media expressions in order not to disparage the image of women in any way.

Looking at all these from a theological perspective, we can see deliberate attempts to treat the female human body as anything but the 'temple of God', of the Holy Spirit. The temple has been desecrated by the rude and powerful male ego. However, with the onset of the women's movement, women themselves have begun to realize the inherent injustice and cruelty in all this.

Jesus' admonition to the Jews to refrain from looking at a woman with lust only goes to prove how sacred he considered the person of women. Paul in his letters severely admonishes those who desecrate the body, be it man or woman. "If anyone destroys the temple of God, God will destroy him" (1Cor 3:9).

Jesus had also a strong word to say against uncleanness in thought and word. "It is what comes out of a person's mouth that defiles a person, and not vice versa" (Mt 15:11). Language is the medium of the human heart and any language that defiles the sacredness of the human person is displeasing to God.

The fact that all over the world women are becoming conscious of this kind of desacralization is a mark of the action of the Spirit. In India, we have also had incidents of women staging protests against pornography and sex films.

3. The Holy Spirit... will teach you all things (Jn 14:25; 16:12-13). The guidance of the Spirit is moving the hearts of many women to discover the truths which have been lying dormant or suppressed in the subconscious for ages. Women across continents, across religions and cultures, in developing as well as developed countries, of different classes and races, are aware of a raising of their own consciousness and self-image by their own efforts or by the help and inspiration of their sisters.

Feminists today are wondering whether the signs of the activity of the Spirit are not visible in the Church and the world already because the unfolding of the same truth seems to take place in different places in different hues and forms. When this kind of emergence of new truths is encountered constantly, there can be no doubt that the action of the Spirit is leading us on in our self-discovery and our liberation.

It is becoming increasingly clear that this process set in motion by the Spirit is leading women on to an authentic vision and expression of their full humanity destined by the Creator for every human being irrespective of gender.

Women are becoming conscious of their own power gifted to them by God, especially that of being co-creators with God in the reproductive process, a responsibility that can neither be over-emphasized nor undervalued.

In the Gospels, Luke begins the tradition that transforms Mary from being merely a historical mother of Jesus, into an independent agent cooperating through her personal will and consent to bring about the messianic event. She became a theological agent in her own right.

4. *Then I saw a new heaven and a new earth (Rev 21:1; Is 65:17). Behold, I make all things new (Rev 21:5).* God's action in this world is open-ended. We are given a foretaste of the shape of things to come, a promise held out in Isaiah and repeated in the Book of Revelation.

For Paul who talks of a new person, the gift of the Spirit is the first part of the redemption of the whole human being, the beginning of a process when a person of faith enters into a mode of existence determined solely by the Spirit. In this new creation, the Spirit will reclaim human beings for God, doing away with all differences, selfish passions and use of power, injustices, and imbalances.

The first Christians experienced that inner transforming power which made them into a perfect community of men and women filled with the gifts of the Spirit, and which made them conclude that this is the power of life, the eschatological Spirit, a foretaste of the future. This future is something which surpasses one's imagination. The prophetic vision handed down to us as future blessings of the Spirit is a vague set of apocalyptic paradoxes as signs of the new times.

THE APOCALYPTIC PARADOXES—SIGNS OF THE NEW TIMES

The wilderness will become a fruitful field (Is 32:15-18). Isaiah says that in the new creation, with the outpouring of the Spirit, the wilderness will become a fruitful field. The wilderness here denoted is the aridness due to the absence of the Spirit, and the fruitfulness is when the earth is once again imbued with the Spirit.

Genesis tells us God gave both man and woman dominion over the earth. An important question nowadays is the question of how women can really share this power and how the whole quality of power could be changed in the process. A good deal of the ecological disaster and the armament race has in fact been caused by a sexual division of labor—women relegated to work of nature (reproduction), men to the production of culture. Participation of women in culture, production, and power cannot just mean numerical equal representation in all walks of life, but a deep transformation of the quality of culture, power and production — a quality based on the reconciliation of culture and nature.

The Chipko Movement is one of the movements initiated by women in the Himachal Pradesh which has caught world attention because women had undertaken the unheard-of task of protecting the forest from being ruthlessly cut down. This is a case in point with regards to the strength of women who not only preserve nature but also conserve it for the future generation.

Then every tear will be wiped away (Rev 7:17; 21:3; Is 25:8). This second paradox is an oft-repeated phrase in the Book of Revelation, the import of which cannot be lost on the women of today. The tears of women who have suffered misery, poverty, ill-treatment and injustice have flowed copiously and unceasingly down the centuries, bringing a feeling of helplessness, rejection and fatalism. In the new creation, the Holy Spirit promises the wiping away of every tear! Tears have been a woman's share, but the wiping away suggests the caring and compassionate hands of others who can remove the harsh situation and provide redress. The Holy Spirit will bring about this change in people's hearts, so that humanity will once more live in harmony and love. Balanced relationships in all spheres of human life will speak loudly of the transforming presence of the Holy Spirit.

The wolf shall dwell with the lamb, and the leopard shall lie down with the kid (Is 11:6ff). In this paradoxical statement, what is set forth is a merging of might and meekness, of power and weakness. But the new creation will bring about a transfusion of the two opposing forces so that once more a harmonious balance is achieved, resulting in a just and balanced order, politically, socially, economically; and where domination of one class, sex or race will disappear. It is possible to see in the peace movements the feminine counterbalancing the masculine, a culture of violence slowly giving way to a movement of peace for everyone.

THE NEED TO EVOLVE NEW MODELS IN THE NEW CREATION

Except for that brief spell in paradise of primordial human beings, the models of human relationships and interaction that have swayed for all these millenia was the matriarchal model in the very early days, followed by the patriarchal to the present day. Humankind has not been able to extricate itself from this uniarchal model as knowledge was so limited in those days and the power over life and nature as understood by the people was predominantly one-sided.

In the earliest cultures unearthed by archeologists, figures of mother goddesses have been found. These small statues depict full-breasted pregnant women. They are generally found without accompanying male symbols for the gods. In this period, the human community was surrounded by nature. Nature itself gave or withheld life. Women gave birth according to mysterious powers that were not understood. As birth-giver, woman became the symbol for all the forces of life. As human knowledge progressed, the power of life as well as control over the forces of nature fell to man's lot. The division of human nature then was classified as the instrumental (male) and the expressive (female). The world soon became man's world with the definite stamp of patriarchy in its structures, beliefs, symbols, norms and patterns of behavior.

Today, the women's movement, poised for bringing about radical changes in our culture, is seen as an impulse of the Spirit, leading us as history-bearers to a new creation marked by total liberation of both men and women. It is rejecting both the patriarchal and the matriarchal models and trying to work out a "diarchal" model for the whole humanity.

This new consciousness or emergence of a new humanity cannot be worked out conceptually or abstractly. It does not occur of our own power. Here the mysterious dynamics of the Holy Spirit will be at work, bringing changes that were inconceivable or impossible. To God nothing is impossible. We have instances in the Bible to prove this point. So, as women, who are carriers of a new vision, our hope is that the Holy Spirit will work in power and mystery towards that new creation.

Methods of Change Envisaged

The methods of change to bring about the new creation would involve, as set forth in the Gospels, both structural on the socio-political level, and imaginal/motivational on the anthropological level.

As agents of change in the Asian setting, we rely strongly on the help of the Holy Spirit to bring about the necessary changes. The promise of the Paraclete was given to us in a three-fold manner:

First, the Paraclete will *walk before us*,[2] leading us on to the truth, to the future; as trailblazer, bringing to mind what the Baptist had to say about God's advent: "Make straight the paths of the Lord" (Mk 1:3). Or in Marxist terminology, the pulling down of unjust structures, leading to an even, classless society. In Jesus' own words, "I have come to cast fire on this earth" (Lk 12:49).

Second, the Paraclete *walking with us* as the comforter *(cum-fortare),* the strengthener, the advocate, the counsellor.

And third, the Paraclete *walking behind us* as the inspirer, the motivational force, the charism-giver.

The only pre-condition necessary for the action of the Spirit is *metanoia,* a change of heart, so that that Spirit can use us pliable instruments for the changes the Spirit wills. All this gives us the strong hope that the coming age will be initiated, installed and supported by the action of the Spirit.

However, the transition period will not be without its painful experiences. There will naturally be the fear of the unknown like the nine-day cenacle experience before the Pentecost. What will be expected of us is a tolerance of ambiguity as humanity goes through a stage of uncertainty and unclarity. As Paul said, "Now we see in a mirror dimly, but then face to face" (1Cor 13:12).

A Concluding Word [3]

We have seen the activity of the Spirit empowering people for life in various human experiences. In the religions, ideologies and cultures of Asia, the Spirit is at work giving life-sustaining and life-enhancing power. "Let us remember that the Spirit does not allow itself to be bound in any way but freely blows" (Jn 3:8).

When people are alienated from their own culture, they are deprived of the fruit of that life-sustaining Spirit. In Asia, the Western culture has trampled on the cultures of the East, bringing about untold sufferings, alienation, and spiritual poverty. Asians have become aware of this and are decrying their being denuded of their spiritual wealth.

The people of Asia have the common experience of the inhuman condition of poverty and oppression. They speak different languages but the Spirit can inspire them to understand one another and unite them in fighting and reclaiming their humanity. Throughout the different countries, people's movements such as the women's movement, youth movement, workers' and peasant movements, etc., are mushrooming. They are manifestations of the Spirit which cuts across gender, language, and national barriers uniting people in common causes. This experience was envisioned by the prophet Joel and fulfilled in the Pentecost experience of the early Christians.

Members of the Church participate in the life and work of the community according to the gifts of the Spirit, so that in a community empowered by the Spirit, all the members participate and share in the responsibility rather than have sharp divisions between clergy and laity, male and female.

In our Asian experience, we see Christians eager to live out the meaning of the Gospel in their struggle for survival. They make use of their special gifts as instruments of liberation. We see the gifts of the Spirit manifested in their determination to go on in spite of all odds, without self-pity, but with a buoyant hope which sustains their struggle. Together with people of other faiths, Christian women and men work towards the attainment of their goal. Power struggle divides people into the powerful and the powerless, but the power of the Spirit unites.

As we reflect on the struggle of people in the Third World, a struggle for a share of human dignity, a struggle in the exercise of responsibility for the creation of a new humanity in a new world, God the Spirit comes as Savior. God is the Spirit stirring over the face of chaos and darkness, creating a world in which there is a mutually life-enhancing relatedness among the various parts.

God the Holy Spirit is moving over the face of the whole earth overcoming forces of chaos and darkness. The Spirit is among people agitating for justice and peace and respect for the whole of creation. In the struggle of the afflicted, the vision of a new day, a new world is coming closer and closer to realization. Those who struggle are not alone for there are those in solidarity with them. Moved by the Spirit, together they become bearers of life, true human life, for the world. Look, listen, feel! The Spirit is renewing the face of the earth!

NOTES

1. *Pro Mundi Vita Bulletin,* "Tourism in Southeast Asia."

2. The terms are borrowed from Katy Millet's Paracletus Paradigm of the Holy Spirit as "walking before us, with us, and behind us."

3. Some of these conclusions come from the "composite paper" on the Holy Spirit. At the Asian Women's Consultation (Manila, November 1985), the participants discussed and critiqued the papers of a particular theme to produce a single "composite paper." See "Proceedings of the Asian Women's Consultation" for complete text.

Part Two

REFLECTING ON ASIAN REALITIES

6

Peace, Unification and Women
I. A Bible Study

Lee Oo Chung (Korea)

Our Bible study theme is "Peace and Unification." I purposely put peace first rather than unification, because I think unification is important for peace, not peace for unification.

This peace is the aspiration of all humankind in this age. Because of today's highly developed science, not only the whole of humanity but all of nature and the earth itself can be destroyed. That is why the German physicist and philosopher Karl Friedrich von Weizsacker said that "peace is a very important condition for our lives in the age of scientific technology." He means that the ultimate survival or destruction of all humankind will depend on whether or not we can achieve world peace. It is already 2,000 years since Jesus said, "Happy are those who work for peace" (Mt 5:9). In Greek the word used for "those who work for peace" is *eirenopoioi,* which means 'make peace'. The implication is that peace cannot be achieved without effort. All of us together have to work hard to make peace.

For example, Korea, which is a small nation, has never waged aggression against any other nation in its five-thousand-year history, yet it has had to fight against large and powerful aggressors such as China, Soviet Russia and Japan. The Korean people have shed their blood and sacrificed their lives to maintain their existence and their land. Still today, Koreans, divided into south and north by the superpowers, are living in the midst of tensions and struggles, surrounded by the superpowers. Because of this first-hand experience, the Korean people's longing for peace is great.

Although we had lived for more than four thousand years as one race, with one language and one culture, our nation was forceably divided into north and south by the superpowers, and then we had the bitter experience of the Korean War. Ever since, we Koreans have been longing more and more for peace and unification.

When Korean people greet each other, they generally use the word *an-nyung* which has a meaning similar to "shalom," the usual greeting among the Hebrews. So Koreans, like the Hebrews, greet each other with a wish for peace, well-being, security and harmony.

As a Korean woman I will try to explain my understanding of peace and unification in the biblical sense. Later, with your question and comments after my presentation, we can hope to get a more holistic view and a better understanding of the true message of the Gospel.

Peace and Unification is the Central Message of Human Salvation

We have chosen for this study Ephesians 2:11-22. In verses 11-13, we see the condition of the Gentiles, who lived without relationship to Christ, and as such they had no part in the covenant. So not only had they no hope for the present life; they also were without hope for the future. The first step, they are told, is reconciliation with God, which is possible through the blood of Christ. In other words, this is a return to the original status of creation.

In verses 14-18, we see a description of the next step, that is, recovery of the relationship among human beings, making a new human community. The dividing wall set up by enmity is broken down, and the divided community is made one through reconciliation with each other. This reconciliation is only possible through the love which Christ showed on the cross.

From verses 19 to 22, we see the new community which is a manifestation of God's family, with Christ as the center. This grows until the whole universe becomes one family, joined together in love and cooperation, until at last the whole universe is God's temple where God lives and rules. This final state is described in Romans 8. All creation groans with pain in its deep longing to be set free from slavery and gain salvation (8:19-23). When this happens, individuals also will enjoy abundant life filled with joy and peace *(plelos)* (15:13). In Ephesians we see that Jesus came to bring universal salvation, and Jesus himself is the message of peace (Eph 2:14).

Jesus saw his own mission as bringing about this kind of state, or salvation. If we look at Luke's Gospel, chapter 10, verses 1-12, Jesus commissions the disciples to complete his mission. He says, "Whenever you go into a house, first say, 'Peace be with this house.'" (10:5) This is different from the daily greeting of the Hebrews to each other. Rather, it was a declaration that "the Kingdom of God has come near you" (10:9). According to the tradition, this is the prophetic declaration of salvation, and this kind of declaration can be found in various forms, in language and parables. It means that God will rule over God's people and all creation, and God's peace will be with them. When the disciples make this declaration, if the householders accept it, they are changed into children of peace who participate in God's work of peacemaking, and thereby all in the house are changed into children of peace and become members of God's Kingdom. This extends to the whole universe, which implies universal salvation.

It is made clear that this is not something which can be arbitrarily accepted or rejected. Rejection brings inevitable judgment. Jesus said, "Whenever you go into a town and are not welcomed, go out in the streets and say, 'Even the dust from your town that sticks to our feet we wipe off against you. But remember that the Kingdom of God has come near you!' I assure you that on the Judgment Day God will show more mercy to Sodom than to that town!" (Lk 10:10-12).

Ephesians describes harmony as peace—first, peace between God and human beings, then peace among human beings, and then peace between human beings and nature. This complete oneness in harmony is the state of God's creation which God looked upon and was very pleased (Gen 1:31). This harmony was broken when human beings ate the fruit of the tree of the knowledge of good and evil. The Korean minjung theologian, Dr. Ahn Byung-Mu, interprets this "fruit of the tree of knowledge of good and evil" as *kong* (公). *Kong* is something which belongs to everyone and is for everyone. Making something which belongs to everyone into private property disobeys God's command, which alienates us from God, thus God's peace is broken (2 Chron 15:1-7). In Leviticus 25:23 we read, "Your land must not be sold on a permanent basis, because you do not own it; it belongs to God, and you are like foreigners who are allowed to make use of it." Dr. Ahn points out that South and North Korea are divided over ideology, and that in order to have dialogue with one another we must find common ground. He finds it through a play on words using two Chinese characters both pronounced "kong", one referring to communism (共), which means fair distribution of all things, and the other (公) one which we use, which refers to ownership by God on behalf of us all.

In the Garden of Eden, when human beings took for themselves alone something which was meant for all humanity, peace was broken and the opposite condition—division and chaos—came into being. Separation from God brought humans further divisions within themselves; they could no longer accept themselves, but were ashamed. They became embarrassed at their nakedness, which was no problem when they were happy with themselves. This was a sign of the brokenness of their mental state and of their personalities. This state of brokenness led to Cain's murder of his brother Abel, and eventually to the destruction of the earth, the very ground of human beings' livelihood. So without God and without hope we continue making division after division in the world. Lamech, a descendant of the murderer Cain, said, "Adah and Zillah, listen to me: I have killed a young man because he struck me. If seven lives are taken to pay for killing Cain, seventy-seven will be taken if anyone kills me" (Gen 4:23-24).

From Genesis 4:22, we find that Lamech's son, Tubal Cain, made all kinds of tools from bronze and iron. We can imagine that it was because of Lamech's confidence in weapons of bronze and iron that he could have the confidence of his life avenged. It reminds us of the U.S. and the U.S.S.R. today, both relying on nuclear weapons and competing for power through the number of weapons. But peace cannot be maintained through the power of weapons. This is made clear by the Bible. We can see it for example in Psalm 33:16-17, Psalm 44:6-7, and Psalm 46:8-9.

Micah 4:3 assures that it is the very opposite of weapons which will bring peace. "God will settle disputes among the great powers near and far. They will hammer their swords into plows and their spears into pruning knives. Nations will never again go to war, never prepare for battle again."

Competition in armaments only brings division, distrust, hatred, competition and revenge. In the Old Testament, the opposite of peace is shedar, meaning division, which includes chaos and alienation and results in war, disease, social class struggle, poverty and natural calamities. All these misfortunes are a result of sin. Looking at the situation in the world since World War II, there have been some 130 wars involving the armies of more than 80 nations, with more than 20 million casualties. And even now war is going on between Iran and Iraq, between Arabs and Israelis, not to mention racial and religious wars in various parts of the world. Added to this is the danger of a major nuclear war between the superpowers which would eliminate tremendous numbers of the population, and could even totally destroy all of civilization.

Looking at Korea itself, because of the division, we experienced the Korean War of 1950-53 in which sisters and brothers killed each other. Then we have the recent Korean Airlines disaster in which 115 persons were killed. When we consider such tragedies, we see clearly that for Korea, peace can only come through unification.

Let us return to Ephesians. Salvation in this divided world can only come through oneness of everything in heaven and on earth. And this can only come through Christ. This providence is planned by God and it is God's secret, *musterion* (Eph 1:9; 3:3-9). To accomplish this purpose, God sent Jesus Christ to earth, and Jesus took all this enmity to himself, changing hatred into love among neighbors, creating a new community (Eph 2:13-22). Ephesians uses one long compound verb, *anakephalaiosasthai,* to express the idea of all divided things becoming one.

This one word is the key to the whole message of Ephesians. The first part, "ana," means to "sum up again," and the main verb, "kephalaioo," the stem of which is "kephale," means "head." So the meaning of this verb is that all things become one under Christ. This does not mean, however, that any part should be sacrificed, or alienated in order to bring all things into one. The real meaning is unity with variety. That is, all the different parts complement each other and cooperate with each other, and in this way we can achieve a more perfect and harmonious world. I believe the author of Ephesians was influenced by Greek philosophy, which interprets "one" *(hen)* as "the ideal perfection." Thus when the basic unit is divided into many, perfection is lost. So Greek philosophy saw perfection beyond plurality in oneness. In Oriental philosophy also, heaven and earth, yin and yang become a harmonious one, where there is perfection, well-being, security, prosperity, fullness, growth, and so forth.

This is a situation similar to what the Bible describes as "shalom." This abolishing of enmity and each complementing the other and seeing neighbors not as "other" but as indispensable partners is exactly the emphasis of feminist theology. In other words, overcoming the enmity between ideologies, systems, sexes, classes, and races and thus forming one peaceful world is our urgent mission task. We have to learn how to live with differences, especially we Koreans both in the South and North. Here, because of our different ideologies and systems, we have feared each other, have built up enemy images and hatred, and piled up weapons to protect ourselves, so this is an even more urgent task for us.

Peace without Justice and Love is Not Peace

Peace in the biblical sense is different from the peace *(pax)* which the Romans used in the political context. Psalm 85 says, "Love and faithfulness will meet; righteousness and peace will embrace" (85:10). And "righteousness will go before the Lord and prepare for him a path of peace" (85:13). Again in Isaiah we find, "Because everyone will do what is right, there will be peace and security forever" (32:17). These passages show that the salvation which comes through God is peace with justice (or righteousness) and love. Peace in the Old Testament includes prosperity, wealth, well-being without anything to block growth (1Sam 20:7; 20:21; 2Sam 17:3; Ps 41:10). Such a state cannot be realized without justice *(tsedek)*. Amos and Micah pointed out the injustice of the powerful and demanded that justice flow like a river. The New Testament describes the suffering of the life of the minjung, through unemployment (Mt 20:1-17), hunger (Lk 16:20), debts (Lk 16:5), illness caused by poverty such as eye disease and deformity (Mk 8:22; Acts 3:2). Furthermore, these minjung suffered from violence under the Roman military governors. Anyone who tried to protest this kind of violence, or who was suspected of trying to organize resistance, was punished ruthlessly. We have a good example of this in Jesus' suffering on the cross. Because of their fear, people were submissive and kept silent; this is the peace we call "pax Romana," and this kind of peace without justice is not peace in the biblical sense. Jesus was sympathetic to the minjung who had to live under such a false peace.

If we look at Exodus we find that God demanded justice based on love (22:21–22; 3:7–8). Deuteronomy 26:5–9 and Nehemiah 9:9–10 show that peace comes from justice and love. When Israel suffered under the Egyptian pharaohs, God heard the cry of God's people (Ex 3:8). In Psalm 72:12 we read, "He rescues the poor who call to him, and those who are needy and neglected." Jesus lived his whole life following this Gospel. In the Old Testament the word *rahamim* or *riham* is used to describe God's love. The stem of this word is "rhm," and the Hebrew word for womb is *rehem* which has the same root. Prof. Phyllis Trible, in her book *God and the Rhetoric of Sexuality*, says that the womb is the vessel and its contents is love. Women who contain life in their bodies, and who care for this life, are more sensitive to God's love. Furthermore, from the sociobiographic perspective, women who have suffered oppression and discrimination down through the years are more sensitive to the pain of the oppressed. Those who trample upon others are unable to feel the pain of those on whom they are trampling. We Third World women, especially Korean women who have lived under foreign occupation, have had to endure great suffering. The patriarchal culture which is based on Confucianism has enforced Korean women's blind obedience and loyalty to men, like that of subjects to the king. Under Japanese rule, nearly 100,000 young women were used as sex objects for the comfort of Japanese soldiers, and many of them died from sex-related disease. Even those who survived were too ashamed to return home. Today, around U.S. military bases and at the pleasure of Japanese male sex-tour groups, young women are selling their bodies. They are mostly from poor families, and they do it to supplement the family earnings, or to help educate their brothers. Those who have been in this kind of situation for a long period commonly suffer from various diseases. Then when they need the help of their family, the family disowns them because they are ashamed. The same fate awaits women who have spent long terms in prison.

Another exploited group are the young women who leave home to work in factories for the same reasons. Recently 22 such young women who were sleeping in a garment factory because they could not afford to rent rooms, died in a fire because the factory owner, fearing they might steal the garments or materials, had closed the shutters and locked them from the outside, making their escape impossible. Such factory owners are an example of those who do not feel the pain of those they are trampling beneath them.

Because women know the pain of suffering people, they were the ones who demonstrated in front of the Anti-Communist Bureau where Park Jong Chul died from torture, and they were the ones who staged the anti-tear gas campaign. If we want to see the corruption and injustice in the society we have to learn about the suffering and feel the suffering of those who are exploited. If we bury the *han* or suffering of such people in order to claim that there is peace, that is not peacemaking.

There are various types of injustice in our society—injustice against laborers, against those in the slum areas, against farmers, against women — while people are crying for justice. If we ignore their cries and do nothing to solve the problems that cause their suffering, claiming that we have peace, we are fooling ourselves. That is not peace, but only "pax Romana."

In Isaiah 11 we read about the fierce lion and the poisonous snakes playing together with children. There we can see equality and partnership. Because of the lack of time I will not give any exegesis of this passage. You might want to discuss later how we could try to achieve such a vision from the world we have described above.

In conclusion: We Koreans living in a divided nation should emphasize our similarities rather than our differences. We have only a few differences, but a very large base of similarities. Yet through all these years we have ignored all these similarities and focused only on our differences, to the extent that North Korea is seen as our most dangerous enemy. As a result, anyone who speaks of peace and unification is labeled by the government as one who is endangering the national security. At the same time he or she is labeled, by conservative Christians, as one who opposes God's will or as communist or pro-communist.

So the division between North and South Korea, and the division within both North and South caused by injustice and lack of love can only be healed when we accept our differences not as cause for inequality or discrimination, but as blessings from God to complement each other.

Women, who have endured discrimination and oppression, are the ones who can see the injustices, and can have understanding and love for those who suffer. We women must become a force for the creation of a new community as God's family. We must begin by reaching out to the suffering people around us, but we must also go beyond, and learn about the suffering, the dreams and the hopes of our sisters and brothers in the North. This will be only a start, but it will be a start on the road to peace and unification.

II. A Theological Reflection

Sun Ai Lee Park (Korea)

Each of the three parts of the title is an independent subject which can be expanded to an inexhaustible length. What I attempt to do here is to deal with peace and national unification issues from a woman's perspective. I will begin with (1) women's lived experience and our new vision, continue with (2) the division of the nation and the effect of the war, go on to the topic of (3) Korean women as the Lamb carrying the sins of the world, and conclude with the issue of (4) peace and women, which will include the Life Movement and Korean feminist theology.

WOMEN'S LIVED EXPERIENCE AND OUR NEW VISION

For thousands of years women have lived a role which is different from that of men. Women have been doing all the work related to their biological functions, and have been alienated from those areas involving language, politics, and academic knowledge of all disciplines; from economically productive activities; and from the spiritual and theological fields. Because of such role distinction, both men and women who should have been whole persons equipped with body and mind, intelligence and feeling, material and spiritual needs, and personal and social lives, have been formed into partial persons with a false definition of norms.

The problem in the formation of partial personhood is the unequal distribution of power, already woven into the formation process itself, let alone into its establishment. When one role is given a greater value than the other, the balance of power is broken and the power dynamics of the powerful and the weak permeates throughout the economic, political and religio-cultural structures of society and family life, forming a graded hierarchical system consisting of those who dominate over others and those who are subordinate. The dynamics of exploitation and victimization is inherent in this system. The male gender has always held the powerful roles during the last five thousand years. Family life, church life, and political affairs in the whole of society have been managed according to patriarchy.

The women's sphere, including the biological, physical and emotional element, has been relegated to a lesser value. Even in traditional theology, women's lived experience has been referred to with contempt as being irrational (nonrational) and non-spiritual, that is, as being purely physical. The exclusion of women's spirituality and the non-recognition of the feminine aspect of God have been the product of both conscious deliberation and unconscious attitude. The image of God the "Father" has been established at the centre of traditional theology.

Nevertheless, through conscientization women are becoming aware of the truth that their lived experience as women has a higher and wholesome value which will be glorified in the eschatological future. The inherent value in a woman's life is to give and nurture life, and to meet the daily physical and spiritual needs of every member of her family, without asking who is more gifted or less meritorious. Women are sensitive to their families' and neighbors' feelings. By the grace of all these virtues women are trained to be more considerate and mindful of others, to play the important role of bringing the human communities together in harmonious unity. Such values are an important part of what our Christian religion has been teaching throughout the ages and of what Jesus Christ has demonstrated in his life, even in the crucifixion and the resurrection. Such values that signify the eschatological glory must be concretized not only among women or solely within the home, but also among men, within the church, and throughout society, in all structures and areas of decision-making.

Humanity faces total destruction by the competitive production of nuclear, chemical, and biochemical weapons. In particular, the Korean peninsula suffers the multi-faceted consequences of division which maintain a deceptive peace whose bargaining objectives are death and destruction. The military tension engaged by a North and South equipped with high-powered war machines, including nuclear weapons, urgently requires the creation of a new way of life, and a system which enables that new way of life. The main substance of this new culture would be absolute respect for life, love, equality, justice and peace for each individual and for all the people.

Isaiah 42:2-4 describes the characteristics of the one who reigns in the new world. "He/She will not cry to lift his/her voice, or make it heard in the street; a bruised reed he/she will not break, and a dimly burning wick he/she will not quench; he/she will faithfully bring forth justice. He/She will not fail or be discouraged till he/she has established justice in the earth and the coastlands wait for his/her law."

The one who will restore justice on the earth is not a violent militaristic authority. He/She is an utterly gentle and considerate mother figure who will not raise his/her voice, lest his/her sleeping baby wake up. His/Her tender heart reaches out even to the bruised reed or dimly burning candle, so that he/she would not dare to terminate the life elements in it, no matter how weak they might be. What a difference from the practice in today's world! Literally and figuratively, the powers-that-be assassinate their political opponents with no regrets. And church politics is no different. Many women face literal and figurative assassination by church authorities. Witch-hunting in the Middle

Ages is a typical case. It is said that 100,000 women were executed in the course of witch-hunting.

The church's modern day witch-hunting is the killing of women's potential and the denial of women's contributions. This kind of psychological and spiritual destruction needs to be voiced aloud, along with the literal murder manifested in cases of suttee,[1] bride burning, and female infanticide practiced in today's India and other places in Asia.

In contrast to these practices, the Messianic figure just described is persistent in bringing forth justice that will be spread to all the coastlands. And the way to realize this justice is non-violent, understanding and loving, with complete respect for each individual's right to life.

The reality of the minjung[2] in the coming kingdom is also described in Luke 6:20-23.

> Blessed are you that hunger now
>   for you shall be satisfied.
> Blessed are you that weep now
>   for you shall laugh.
> Blessed are you when men hate you
>   and when they execute you and cast out your name
>   as evil, on account of the Son of man!
> Rejoice in that day, and leap for joy,
> For behold, your reward is great in heaven;
> For so their fathers did to the Prophets.

When the powers of oppression and exploitation come to an end and the new kingdom is realized, all the exploited and victimized will have their rights restored to them as equal children of God. Among the victimized and exploited, women are the greatest number. If they persist in believing in and working toward the actualization of the Christ event, women, even if they are hated by men and excluded and reviled by them, will be rewarded greatly in the new day!

When just political power takes charge of the affairs of the world, respecting meekness, love, life, righteousness and peace, overcoming the enormous military power and violence of exploitation, a new day will arrive when people can enjoy life in a totally different cultural setting with an entirely different value system. If muscular violence is the symbol of patriarchy, the alternative value and culture must be that of a feminist spirituality which is based on women's lived experience.

In the case of Korea, this new day must be established by the power of the oppressed and exploited people themselves. The oppression comes from the big powers in the international political and economic scene as well as from the domestic elites. For Korean women there is the added oppression of sexual discrimination. True unification will be made when all these forces of oppression and exploitation are overcome and a genuine reconciliation is made among people from all walks of life, and between the sexes in mutual respect and love of the other.

THE DIVISION OF THE NATION AND THE EFFECTS OF THE WAR

The division of the land and people of Korea is a typical case of the powerless who suffer a tragic destiny imposed on them by the ideological and military conflict of the superpowers. Religiously speaking, those in power, impregnated by their original sin of desiring to conquer and dominate others, subduing them and keeping them under categories of their own images, give birth to many suffering lambs. Korea as the prototype has become "the lamb carrying the sins of the world." This naming appears in the statement of peace and justice issued by the National Council of Churches in Korea (NCCK) in February 1988 and also in a study of the Gospel of Mark by Professor Ahn Byung Mu, the leading Minjung theologian in Korea.

Biblically speaking, an atoning lamb carries two significations: suffering and redemption. In the case of Korea we have heard innumerable stories and seen countless realities of suffering. Throughout Korea's long national history of domination and subjugation, redemptive effort towards freedom has continuously been made by the Minjung (people's) Movement. Countless numbers of young people and others have been struggling for justice and freedom. Redemptive work is imminent in our history through their actions. But the eschatological reign of God is an historical task which is yet to come.

As major characteristics of the Third World, one can point out political dictatorship, economic and cultural poverty of the ordinary people due to exploitation by both external powers and internal elites, and the overall cultural colonization which affects the value system of the people.

The economic development and the efforts to recover their national culture made by the Korean people during the last two to three decades are rightfully a source of pride. But, on the other hand, many minjung, especially minjung women and children, have not been enjoying an equal distribution of the fruits of that effort. Politically, economic development and fear of invasion by the communist North have been used to justify the anti-communist policies of the military dictatorial regimes. In other words, in order to enforce anti-communism, the freedom of the people and the principles of democracy have had to be sacrificed. In the absence of a positive ideology, only a negative ideology has been at work, namely, anti-communism. When negative anti-communism is placed at the centre of national policy with no room for a positive way of practicing democracy, the whole national life and the people's mode of thinking and behavior are bound to be affected. In order to negate the negative, people are actively engaged in an anti-government, anti-military, and anti-authoritarian democratization movement.

The division of Korea also brought on the infamous Korean War of 1950-53. The visible and invisible side-effects still grip the life of the people. The NCCK statement describes the casualties of the war as follows:

The Korean War of June 25, 1950 produced the tragedy of fratricide and polarized the international conflict. More bombs were thrown in Korea by the U.N. forces than all the bombs used all over Europe during World War II, making the Korean peninsula totally devastated. The death toll during this war were 220,000 from the South Korean Army, more than 600,000 from the North Korean Army, one million from the Chinese Army, 140,000 from the U.S. Army, and 16,000 from the U.N. Army. Including the dead by sickness during the war, the total military sacrifice amounts to 2,500,000. Together with 500,000 South Korean civilians and 3,000,000 North Koreans, the blood of 6,000,000 was spilt on this land.[3]

The number of human casualties shown here is enormous. And the most striking fact is that civilian casualty is much greater than all of the armed forces combined, and the number of bombs used on Korea is much greater than all the bombs used on European soil during World War II. One cannot but suspect the reality of racism in the policy of this war.

Both in the South and in the North, the material destruction of the war has been restored as part of each side's development effort. However, the psychological effect on the whole people is very deep. People are afraid of the possibility of the recurrence of another war, and the dictators make use of the psychology of fear on the people, manipulating the people's minds in order to maintain their own power.

KOREAN WOMEN AS THE LAMB CARRYING THE SINS OF THE WORLD

All the wars fought in the post-World War II era took place in Third World countries. Judging from the fact that the Korean soil and people were pushed into being the local contractors in the superpowers' ideological warfare, one can say that the Korean War was the event that has turned the country into a sacrificial lamb that carries the sins of the world.

This war did not end in a treaty of peace but only in a truce. The wall between the North and South has become higher as it has sown the seed of hatred and enmity among the people of both the North and the South. Ten million of the total sixty million Koreans have become victims of separated families.[4] Yet neither government has shown any concern for the solution of this grave problem. Nor can the people express their desire for reunion of families in any political forum. Only recently, with the rise of the reunification movement among the people of South Korea, has this issue, along with other issues, begun to surface in public forum.

This division also became a rationale for the expansion of militarism. The heavily increasing arms race between the two parties, and especially the nuclear weapons in stock under the U.S. command in the South and along the Soviet border line, threaten the peace of Northeast Asia and the whole world.

As the problems of the Korean peninsula were not caused by Koreans alone, so the solution must also be worked out from many angles, for the effect to be far-reaching. The famous Korean poet Kim Chi Ha has said that the solution for the Korean peninsula will be a light to all Third World countries. Theologically speaking, the suffering lamb that carries the sins of the world is called to be the lamb of redemption that redeems the sins of the world.

Among the Korean minjung who are burdened by international and domestic exploitation, women carry the greater load. In addition to the overall load that they carry as Koreans and as poor, they also carry the burden of their men. Many women are victims of sexual violation, rape, prostitution, physical and psychological violence by their men who have need of an emotional outlet for their social frustration. Moreover, the women dedicate themselves in rewardless domestic labor and sacrificial service in all aspects of life. In return they are often abandoned by the men. In Korea, whatever is defined as women's work is regarded as worthless.

As our national life faces all kinds of insecurity and the violent consequences of the division of the Korean peninsula, women, despite everything, are the ones who carry out the role of peace- and harmony-makers in the homes, in the work place, and in the churches. Korean women therefore are the most suffering of the suffering lambs, carrying out the role of imminent and potential eschatological redemption for all. For the final redemption that is yet to come, we women need to be aware of our triple and quadruple oppression. Such awareness will enable us to use the collective power of sisterhood and peoplehood to overcome all our burdens and be free. Our freedom will then transform us into a new creation not only as individuals but also as a people and as church.

PEACE AND WOMEN

Because women give birth to life, nurture and sustain life, we feel repulsion to any destruction. Patriarchal male culture is founded on power dynamics in which violence is a mighty currency and the survival of the fittest is the principle whereby the stronger takes over the weaker. Thus conflict and strife never end between individuals, groups, local communities, and nations, leading to a reality in which innumerable lives are destroyed in wars. The creator God calls forth a life movement, the enhancement of life and urging opposition to the power of death. The Life Movement takes the form of an anti-war, anti-nuclear peace movement. When women's movements progress to a deeper level, they are bound to become a peace movement, too. As peace and life have been important concerns of Korean women's movements, one must say we are on the right track.

The division of the Korean peninsula not only destroys the justice of God and the wholeness of national life but also breeds insecurity. Polarizing conflict, war and mutual hatred are the consequences of the division and portends further violence and death. The reality of ten million separated family members signifies so many people's pain and suffering; it also means the destruction and annihilation of so many women's life-long work and dedication. It means taking away from them all that they have valued and hold dearest to them. The reality of a political dictatorship and the reality of separated families with no effort towards any solution have their root and origin in patriarchal culture.

The Korean women's movement, born out of pain and suffering from the multi-faceted effects of national division, has already participated in the march towards peaceful national reunification, even if there was no verbal expression or consciousness of it as such in the past. The fact is that we have been working for the survival issues of grassroots women: for peace and love, democratization, and human rights. All our actions were political and part of history-making. The unification movement which is becoming strong and forceful in today's Korea has solid roots in the trend towards democratization and in the human rights movement of the last three decades.

At the same time a new stage is unfolding before us in which the unification issue is being taken up as the political action of the Korean women's movement. Now that we have started to theologize on the theme from the women's perspective, and various action plans of conscientization and a meeting of women from both the North and the South are being undertaken, concrete strategies and realistic actions towards reunification must take place.

Korean people envision reunification of the nation in a peaceful way. The experience of the Korean war from 1950 to 1953 was totally negative. Moreover, all the conscientized people, especially the students, are fully aware of the escalating militarism on both sides and of the nuclear weapons deployment in South Korea under the U.S. military command.

The most outstanding slogans of the student movement and of the democratization and unification movement in today's Korea are anti-war, anti-nuclear, and anti-U.S.A. The self-evident reading of these slogans explicates that the means of unification they envisage are not by war, especially not by the use of nuclear weapons. The people are also aware that the U.S.A. is the most powerful obstacle to the democratization and unification of Korea and that a self-reliant people's movement alone can achieve these objectives.

Within this general trend in Korean national life, Christian women who are willing to make a positive contribution toward a peaceful unification of the nation must develop a theology of peace from the women's perspective based on the historical context. The trinitarian approach to democratization, unification, and women's liberation must be the working principle and the paradigm. It still maintains the underlying trinitarian principle of *minjok* (the national people), *minjung* (the oppressed masses), and *minju* (democracy) of the late seventies and early eighties. On the solid basis of the Three-Min Movement, the newly-verbalized unification issue and the women's issue must be surfaced to form a trinitarian paradigm of feminist theology of today— tackling the issues of democratization, unification and women's liberation simultaneously. If one can accept that democratization and unification are the inseparable way to ultimate national independence and freedom, then it follows that one should also accept that women's liberation and dignity should also be worked out within this great task of national independence.

The writers of the Bible and the traditional church theologians were men whose patriarchal values have permeated the life of the church. Many women abandoned the Bible and left the church in protest. However, many more remain in the church, searching for the mother images and feminine images of God, and developing a theology from women's perspective.

Feminist theology is developed on the basis of women's lived experience. The experience includes discrimination against them for being women and their unique life experiences as women. From the situation of being ignored and forsaken for thousands of years, women affirm their being and find images of God which they can identify with and use in their theologizing. This women's movement has as its ultimate goal to bring about inclusion of a value system based on the equality of both sexes, inclusive symbols, liturgies, and ways of life. When we read the Bible it is necessary to look at it with feminist suspicion as Elisabeth Schussler Fiorenza maintains,[5] but we must also be ready to accept truth and prophetic principles which are applicable to both women and men. Rosemary Ruether points to the invariables and variables in the Bible. As an invariable, she points to the prophetic principle which can be applied to the variable realities.[6] Even if the prophetic writings did not have women's issues in mind, women of today can apply the prophetic principles of justice to women's situations. The Korean Minjung Movement, the women's movement, and all the other kinds of renewal movements are struggles to be free from the domination of external and internal powers, including political, economic, and cultural domination of the more powerful over the powerless. In order to become the true images of God and to be faithful to the creative intent of the Creator, the existing authorities of dominant powers must be questioned in light of equality, justice, unity, and peace.

Among all the inclusive biblical themes, peace is one of the most prominent and most representative of women's life. The Catholic Bishops of the U.S.A. summarize biblical peace in their "Pastoral Letter on War and Peace" as follows:

> Several points must be taken into account in considering the image of peace in the Old Testament. First, all notions of peace must be understood in light of Israel's relation to God. Peace is always seen as a gift from God and as fruit of God's saving activity. Secondly, the individual's personal peace is not greatly stressed. The well-being and freedom from fear which result from God's love are viewed primarily as they pertain to the community and its unity and harmony. Furthermore, this unity and harmony extend to all of creation; true peace implies a restoration of the right order not just among peoples but within all of creation. Third, while the images of war and the warrior God become less dominant as a more profound and complex understanding of God is presented in the texts, the images of peace and the demands upon the people of covenantal

fidelity to true peace grow more urgent and more developed.[7]

Patriarchy produces a graded system, classism and racism among people as well as inequality and conflict in the human community. Unity and harmony of the community can only be brought about by another culture which is not patriarchal. This new culture would enhance equality, offer a less structured life and allow for genuine democratic participation of its members. This is like a mother who loves, clothes, and feeds all of her children equally regardless of differences in intelligence, outward appearance, etc. She finds a hidden pearl in a child of whom no one else speaks highly in any way.

Women experience the monthly rhythm of menses and the full bloom of life through pregnancy; they give birth to new lives which they nurture. They meet the physical and emotional needs of their families in everyday life situations. Through their biological role they experience true harmony with nature, which approaches the biblical sense of peace. When women are given the freedom of holistic expression in their life (including in the educational process and in their social participation), their theology of peace will be holistic and truly biblical.

In 1985 the International Affairs Desk of the Christian Conference of Asia had an international conference on Peace in Asia. During this conference an analysis of the Chinese ideogram that stands for peace was made (平和). It is made up of two symbols. The first one is (平) which stands for balance. The balance has two equal weights (平). The second symbol (和) means harmony. The first radical symbol (禾) signifies grains and the second (口) mouth. Harmony is made when the mouth goes together with the grain. The combination of the two symbols means that peace is realized when every mouth is fed evenly. Here the spirituality of peace embraces materialism. And women know what this means from their hearts and lives. They don't have to attend an international conference to find it out. The issue at stake here is that the spirituality of women's lived experiences has been ignored and belittled throughout Christian history despite the fact that the era of the forbidden tree was terminated a long time ago. Have not both Adam and Eve tasted of the fruit of knowledge? Adam became knowledgeable about God, the world, and himself; but so did Eve. What she needs is a forum to speak out what she knows of her experience of life and peace.

Women of the world have been living out peace as expressed in the Chinese ideogram. Instead of being belittled, their skill of making peace by providing food for every mouth in the family should be extended to local, national, and international communities. Equipped with political skills, backed by the constituency of the women's movement, and experienced in feminist leadership, women will be able to bring peace to the divided, wartorn, and heavily militarized Korean peninsula. However, given the complex international factors which have been shaping Korea's destiny, the strong support and enabling work of international solidarity are also required.

Isaiah 48:18 describes peace as follows: 'O that you had hearkened to my commandment; Then your peace would have been like a river, and your righteousness like the waves of the Sea.'' Peace here is preceded by justice and doing justice means to keep in mind God's command. God's command here applies both to men and women. The obligation is to keep the command as well as to have the privilege of enjoying peace.

The consequence of keeping God's command belongs equally to men and women. However, under patriarchal political and economic structures, women's obligation is limited to the family, whereas men hold positions of authority in the public sphere where the exercise of power affects the whole society. Unfortunately, the orientation of such men is basically androcentric, since they do not have the basic experience of sharing and directly providing for the daily needs of the family, the basic unit of human community. It is natural that the authorities and hierarchies which dwell on theoretical and structural questions become utterly impotent when it comes to heart, hand, and foot matters. Therefore, the power that is constituted by an androcentric outlook and its ways can hardly be expected to provide an even distribution of food and other material needs to their people in order to bring about the peace which the Chinese ideogram signifies.

CONCLUSIONS

Authentic peace can only be achieved with true equality between men and women. But this equality must start from family life in the nitty-gritty work of household chores and child-rearing. When these are shared between men and women, men can attain the higher values in life, while women can accumulate the social experience and political skills which they have hitherto been deprived of and which are necessary in order for them to hold leadership positions in the broader society. The exercise of power from women's perspective can help towards the change in the present structures.

The women's power which can destroy the walls of sexual discrimination between men and women can also destroy the oppressions and exploitative mechanism of internal and external powers. The root of all these divisions is patriarchy which must be uprooted to achieve peace and liberation. For the organized women's movement in Korea, therefore, the road to national democratization and unification and the road to women's liberation are the irrefutable means towards a lasting peace and total human liberation.

NOTES

1. An ancient custom of India. The widow is burnt with the dead body of her husband on his funeral pyre. Also spelled sati.

2. Masses of deprived, exploited, oppressed and alienated people.

3. Declaration of the National Council of Churches in Korea on Unification and Peace of the Nation, February 1988. Published by the National Council of Churches in Korea: 5.

4. Lee Hyo Jai, "The Divided Society and Women," *In God's Image,* ed. Sun Ai Park (June 1988): 7-10.

5. Elisabeth Schussler Fiorenza, "The Will to Choose or to Reject: Continuing Our Critical Work," in *Feminist Interpretation of the Bible,* ed. Letty M. Russell (Philadelphia: The Westminster Press, 1985), 125-136.

6. Rosemary Radford Ruether, "Feminist Interpretation: A Method of Correlation," *Feminist Interpretation of the Bible,* ed. Letty M. Russell (Philadelphia: Westminster Press, 1985), 111-124.

7. Catholic Bishops of U.S.A., "Pastoral Letter on War and Peace," 11.

7

Biblical Concept of Human Sexuality: Challenge to Tourism

Elizabeth Dominguez (Philippines)

I am really delighted to have this opportunity of participating in the conference that is going to deal with women and tourism. Specifically we are going to be addressing the tragedy that is prostitution. At the same time, I will try to cover the four topics that have been assigned to me.

May I begin by inviting you to rediscover the biblical concept of sex, of human sexuality. I do not know if it is just in the Philippines that there is that attitude toward sex which views it as dirty, as something we should not be talking about openly if we are to be decent, reserved, and civilized. It is not for public discussion. Our discussion today takes a different route and starts from a different presupposition. For we believe it will help us in our own understanding of the Christian faith and our own struggles to rediscover the concept of sex in the Scriptures.

CREATED IN THE IMAGE OF GOD

In Genesis 1:26ff, we have a claim made about human beings which is the highest commendation for humanity ever, and that is the description of human beings as created in the image of God. Right after Adam is described as created in the image of God, it is claimed that Adam is created male and female, so that the highest commendation used for humanity, made in the image of God, is immediately associated with human sexuality.

But what happened to the situation described in Genesis 1? We know that the male portion of humanity has monopolized that description for itself so that "man" came to be understood as *male* instead of Adam which is specifically described as *male* and *female*. How anyone could miss the point by reading very simply, very faithfully, what is written there, and how anyone could interpret the male as the one described as created in the image of God,

I have the hardest time understanding because it is clearly stated in the passage that God created them male and female.

So Adam means both male and female, the human family. It has been suggested a number of times that instead of translating the Hebrew Adam to 'man', it is better to translate it as 'humanity' or 'humankind' so that it would definitely include male and female. We know that Saint Paul himself, in 1Corinthians 11, understood Genesis 1:26 to be talking about a male person. But if you deal with 1Corinthians 11 more deeply, you will soon find out that Paul is talking about proper attire in worship and he concentrates more on women. Concerned about addressing a way of life, a manner of clothing and attiring people, Paul ends up reading Scriptures in such a way that women are considered as second rate, as second class, as secondary creation. This is how Paul understood and elucidated Genesis 1:26.

Our way of life and cultural inheritance make us read texts in a particular way. It is a matter of really reading more carefully and rediscovering what is expressed there. As far as this issue on human sexuality is concerned, women have a lot to contribute because the misreading of the Bible has victimized women and such victimization, in turn, has been sanctified by quotations from Scriptures. So we hope that women, as those victimized by the misreading of Scripture, will play the role of rediscovering authentic scriptural tradition.

What then is human sexuality according to Genesis 1:26ff? If human sexuality is immediately associated with the fact that humanity is created in the image of God, then human sexuality is to remind us that humanity must go on. Humanity is given by God and the responsibility of perpetuating itself, multiplying, continuing on, remains. It is worth preserving because humanity has been endowed by God with the responsibility of managing the rest of creation. Human sexuality is for human beings to gain numerical strength over beasts and other creatures because humanity is chosen by God to play the very important responsibility of managing the rest of creation.

For humanity to be described "male and female" should also make us aware that humanity is meant to be all-inclusive. "Male and female" is still the most inclusive description of humanity. If you describe humanity as black and white you always have the brown and yellow that would be excluded. If you describe humanity as rich and poor you leave out the middle class. But if you describe humanity as male and female nobody is excluded. So the description of humanity as created in the image of God, "male and female," reminds us that for humanity to reflect the glory of God humanity must be seriously inclusive. To create and perpetuate a situation out of the distinction between male and female where the female is considered as second rate or an "assisting" sex is already destroying that inclusiveness. "Male and female" emphasizes that it is total humanity that expresses the image of God.

The last detail I would like to reflect on in Genesis 1:26ff is that the description of Adam as "male and female" stresses that basically we are made for community. It is not individual Christians who reflect the glory of God; it is rather Christians who decide to belong together as a community and to reflect the glory of God in their life together as community. I think it distorts the meaning of human sexuality to think of "image of God" as reflecting the qualities of individual persons rather than a way of living with one another. It is in the way we live with one another that we reflect that there is an empowering God, a forgiving God, a God who continues to employ us and renew us together. It is in our fellowship together, in our acceptance of each other, in our confidence in each other, in our belief that problems are not going to be solved by individuals, not even by individual nations but by all peoples working together. All the things that communities of persons do together reflect the glory of God. That is what it means to be created in God's image.

THE CREATION STORIES

The first chapter of Genesis is one story of creation. It is not the only creation story. In the second chapter of Genesis we have the second story of creation. In this second story, human sexuality is commented on a little bit more. Yes, Adam in Genesis 2 means "male." However, it is important for us to remember that while Adam in Genesis 2 means "male," the word "Adam" is taken from a Hebrew word adama which means "soil"/"ground." It is a very humbling reminder because "Eve" is taken from a Hebrew word which means "mother of the living." So Adam is "ground" (male), while Eve means "mother of the living" (female).

I do not know how you can derive out of Genesis 2 the understanding that "man " or "male" is intended to be superior to "woman" or "female" in the order of creation. It is said that male is superior because the male is created first and the female is created out of a rib derived from the male. Let me share one interpretation of this with you. The male, Adam, is created out of the ground and the female, Eve, is created out of the rib. Definitely, the rib is of a higher order of creation than the ground. But actually, if we look at the whole story of Adam and Eve in Genesis 2, this is really how it goes:

The male was created first, but he felt so alone despite the beasts that were created for him. Beasts can also keep us company as you who are pet lovers know. So beasts were created in order to overcome aloneness but the man with all the beasts could not overcome his aloneness. In other words, aloneness can only be overcome by the company of an equal. Beasts are not the equal of man so woman was created in order to give real company and real companionship that can only be enjoyed by equals, not by superiors and inferiors.

That is how I look at chapter 2. When Eve was created, Scripture says, "a man leaves mother and father to become one with her." Sex, therefore, is God's provision for the deepest communion, and this deepest communion can only take place if it is a communion between equals. The natural closeness of a human being to mother and father is transcended by a relationship which is decided and entered into in freedom and in this relationship the hope is for deepest communion. Sexuality therefore is a gift of God for highest communion of human beings.

It would be important for us to note that the second story of creation

85

is dated in the time of Solomon. Solomon is known for having many concubines, although in Jewish tradition he is rather remembered as the one who built the Temple. Our Scripture records Solomon as acquiring many concubines. Actually this was a practice which was a way of sealing alliances between nations. So the rulers of a nation can have as concubines the daughters of the kings of other nations in order to seal a political alliance. So marriages and women were used for political alliances. In Genesis 2, we most likely have a protest against this practice of using women for any kind of purpose because sex is intended by God for highest communion.

One Old Testament book, *Song of Songs,* is actually a collection of very erotic poetry that celebrates human sexuality as God's gift to humanity. Unfortunately, all this became allegorized in both the Jewish heritage and Christian tradition so we tend to forget that the book is actually about the beauty of human sexuality and the possibility of deep communion, and that erotic love is in the very plan of God.

THE SO-CALLED INFERIORITY OF THE FEMALE

Let us now look at the place of human sexuality in our lives as human beings and address the concept that femaleness is weakness and maleness is strength and the issue of women being ruled by men. Genesis 3, where you have a specific description of women undergoing the experience of childbearing and being lorded over by her husband and of men enjoying the fruits of his labor but always struggling and not harvesting the fruits, is actually the description of "the fall." It is the portrayal of the separation of human beings from God because they want to be "like God." Take note of Genesis 3:4 "If you eat the fruit of the tree you will be as wise as God." You will know what is evil and good and you will be as wise as God. There was this desire to be like God which results in alienation. This is what we call "the fall."

The cause of the fall was the human desire to be like God. Human beings should desire to be true human beings, not to be beasts or to be God. The desire to be like God is at the root of sin. So we have the fall. That is where the description that woman is going to be ruled over by her husband is found. The man on the other hand is going to work hard but there will be no fruit for that labor.

How in the world did we make the description of the fall as our typical description of woman-man relationship, as if we want to be condemned to that state of things? We women should rediscover our true heritage and discover a genuine, humanizing relationship between the two sexes that would make us more human rather than brutal towards one another.

PROSTITUTION IN THE OLD TESTAMENT

Let me now turn to the next sub-topic which is prostitution in the society of the Hebrew people. Much of what I have written down to say has already been said by our sister who gave the morning's message. So some of it I will just mention in passing but first of all, I want to clarify that prostitution is rendering sex service for hire. So it is a commercialization of sex. Sex which has been given to us by God for deepest communion is now an instrument for money. In prostitution, the sexual relationship is not a binding relationship. There is no commitment in that relationship and while human beings are supposed to be for communion, for deepest relationship, in prostitution there is nothing of that. As our sister preacher reminded us, we have two prostitutes in the Old Testament that are remembered in Hebrew tradition for their virtues.

Tamar is remembered for her virtue (Gen 38). What was her virtue? In the Hebrew practice of levirate marriage, when the husband dies without an heir, without a son, then the wife is to bear a child for her husband via the husband's brother. That is levirate marriage. There is one good thing about levirate marriage and one bad thing. The good thing is that it reminds us that the living have responsibility for the dead. When a person dies the person continues to make a claim on us. When a husband dies and there is no heir, then the wife bears an heir for him just the same. Caring for the dead allows the dead to have claims on us. I think there is something for us to reflect on in relation to this issue. But the bad thing about it is that the wife must bear an heir for the late husband so that this is a bondage to the relationship even after death. Tamar takes the responsibility very seriously but the father of her husband tries to get out of it by not arranging for the third brother of Tamar's husband to help her bear the heir. Tamar insists on the practice, and therefore, she disguises herself as a prostitute and as the story goes, the father-in-law of Tamar himself uses her, not knowing that she is his daughter-in-law. As a result, she conceives. Before she can be stoned to death she reveals the evidence that it was her own father-in-law who did it to her. The conclusion of the story is that Tamar is proved to be more righteous than her father-in-law because she insisted on the levirate marriage.

The story of Rahab reminds me of many Philippine prostitutes. If you read the story in Joshua 2, it is very specific there that Rahab negotiated with the Israelite conquerors. Israelites were getting into Canaan as conquerors. They went into Canaan with a new way of community life, the community life of equals rather than of kings and slaves. When Rahab negotiated with the Israelite conquerors, she negotiated for the security of her family. She says: "We have heard so much of how strong you are as fighters and we have no way of getting away from you. I want to make sure that I will be able to secure my father, my mother, my brothers and sisters, so I want to negotiate with you." It is interesting because as the dialogue goes on, the Israelites, the Hebrew soldiers, would say, "Yes, you are going to be secure with your father, your mother and your brothers." *Sisters* are omitted. It is a startling omission since Rahab mentions father, mother, brothers and *sisters.* I wanted to take note of this because I am reminded of Philippine prostitutes. So many of them are engaged in this trade precisely for the security of their families: father, mother, brothers, sisters and even daughters. This is the virtue of Rahab, the virtue of Rahab was that she was willing to do what was needed for the sake of her family. We ought to be able to understand that ourselves for we all belong to a family.

In the Old Testament, we have texts which specifically condemn prostitution. Leviticus 19:29 prohibits a Hebrew family from having a daughter given up to prostitution. In Deuteronomy 23:18, hiring a harlot is unfit as an offering to God. I just like to point out, however, that in both Leviticus and Deuteronomy, there is still the spirit of Jewish superiority over Gentiles. When the families are appealed to not to allow their daughters to be prostitutes, this applied only to Jews. There was no prohibition for the Gentiles. So while condemning an act for some, it is deemed good for others.

The text in Amos 2:7 was also referred to by our preacher this morning. I just want to note again that the society in which Amos lived was a materially progressive society. It was a very rich society. In fact, it was the highest economic standard that the Hebrew people ever reached. It is tragic, however, when material development is accompanied by the continuous degradation of women. What is happening in modern society was happening in Amos' time. In the Book of Amos, the poor are sold for a pair of shoes, while the upper class sleep in beds of ivory and have winter and summer houses. You also have a father and son using the same maiden. In other words, prostitution became a matter of fact and the prophet Amos not only criticized it; he vehemently condemned it.

In the Old Testament there was the practice of concubines. Barren women would use their housemaids to enable their husband to have a son, as seen in the stories of Rachel and Leah and of Sarah and Abraham. Sarah uses her maid. For me this is a very good illustration of women from a higher economic class exploiting their own sex group. You have Rachel and Leah making use of their housemaids in the rivalry over the affection of Jacob. So many women of our time share that kind of attitude, being so concerned about their status and acceptability within their own class that they are not hurt or pained by the human degradation of sisters belonging to another class. We have it in the Old Testament times and we have it now in the twentieth century.

Another group of women who easily became prostitutes were, of course, women who belonged to conquered nations. In Joel 3:1-3 and Lamentations 5, there are descriptions of how women became the symbol of defeat for Israel by the way they were treated by conquerors. It must have been a real experience of power on the part of men of conquering nations to have women at their disposal. By the way, in Joel 3:1-3, it is not only women who were overpowered by conquering men but also the little boys of the conquered nations. This again reminds me very much of the situation in my own country. I am sure those of you who have been to the Philippines have heard that where you have beautiful surroundings enjoyed by tourists, you also have male children ranging from age six to fourteen, sometimes up to twenty, at the service of tourists. In other words, when you have the exploitation of women, very often it is also accompanied by the exploitation of other human beings who, because of their economic status or age are considered at the disposal of others who are stronger and who can have power over them. In the end, prostitution is really an instance of human beings using and controlling other human beings, though it be under the guise of tourism or the rest and recreation of military personnel.

PROSTITUTION IN THE NEW TESTAMENT

The Gospels give us a picture of Jesus' treatment of prostitutes. Let me mention first of all the story of the woman of Samaria. In the story Jesus engages a prostitute in a conversation, in a dialogue, in fact, in a very serious theological discussion. Jesus initiates the conversation by asking the woman for a drink of water. He was in need. In this story Jesus dignifies the Samaritan woman by taking her seriously as a human being capable of having a conversation with him and not as a human being that needs to be rescued, like so many of us are wont to do because we feel good when we do the rescuing. It puts us in a better position.

The woman is taken seriously and the woman proves herself capable of such a discussion. Out of that dialogue Jesus produces the most effective evangelist because the woman's testimony converts a whole Samaritan village and their confession is beautiful. When one says "Jesus is Messiah," that is very Jewish but the Samaritans are attributed with a beautiful confession that "Jesus is Savior of the world." This from people supposed to be heretics from the Jewish point of view! This confession was made by the people in a village evangelized by a woman prostitute. How many of us take prostitutes seriously as fellow human beings who are capable of discussing theological issues, of analyzing what is going on, of evangelizing a village?

Another picture we get of Jesus' treatment of the prostitutes is seen in John 7:53-8:1. It is a story of a woman caught in the act of adultery. I cannot help but make a comment: how can adultery be committed by a woman alone? It is just the woman caught in adultery; there is no mention of any man. The men are there to stone the woman. Our male translators and male preservers of tradition find it all right to keep the record like that. The immortal statement of Jesus in concluding the issue is this: "Let him who is without sin cast the first stone." In other words, in the eyes of Jesus, we do not have a hierarchical arrangement of sin. Some of us feel proud to claim that we only have sins of pride or of being over-decent. But when Jesus said "let him who is without sin cast the first stone," he condemns all sin and not the woman.

Another statement of Jesus is to religious leaders, Pharisees, Sadducees and Scribes, but that should include us too as leaders in our churches. Jesus said, "Thieves, prostitutes and harlots will go to heaven ahead of you." This reminds me of a story of one exceptionally beautiful Filipina prostitute who had a relationship with a rich Filipino technocrat. The Harvard trained technocrat was so attracted to this prostitute that he offered her marriage. But the prostitute did not want to marry him. So he said, "Look, I'm offering you a new future and a decent life. That is what I am offering you in spite of everything. I will forget everything." The answer of this prostitute was this: "You know I sell my body but do you realize that you are selling your soul by playing into the hands of multinationals that rape our natural and human resources?" The woman is saying, in effect, that offering her a decent future was incompatible with the act of robbing the Filipino people, a graver sin. "I sell my body, you sell your soul."

We do not have to be technocrats to participate in the guilt of such a man. We are given the privilege to mingle with people coming from different countries to talk about issues of tourism and prostitution. If we do not feel responsible for doing something about the degradation of women of another economic class who have internalized their degradation and humiliation and have accepted these as part of their life, I do not think we are less guilty than that Filipino technocrat.

OUR TASK

I am supposed to conclude with some remarks on the Christian woman's task in countries where women are degraded as prostitutes. A primary task is the education of women—prostitutes and non-prostitutes alike—so that prostitutes can be acknowledged as the victims of a social order in which women have been taken as commodities. Let us all graduate from moralism. Let us not be that ambitious. Is it our goal to be moral persons, decent persons or to be persons who know how to give or enhance human life in others? As long as we want to be moralistic I do not think there could be any genuine communication between the prostitutes and ourselves. This is possible only if we come to them with an understanding and analysis of society. Why is it that we are where we are? Why has material progress not heightened the value of human dignity? Why is it that the more we improve materially, the more we behave like beasts? It is like the tower of Babel where human beings built a tower so that they could go up where they thought God was. The tower was destroyed and they instead got the opposite result. In our time, we are supposed to have progressed in many ways but it is also in our time when human beings have been degraded and humiliated so seriously.

As I suggested in relation to the story of Jesus' treatment of the Samaritan woman, having a dialogue with women who have "strayed" has to be a dialogue among equals. If we cannot take them as equals, then that is where prayers should come in. Let us pray that God will put into our consciousness the kind of attitude that Jesus himself had, so that we can stop merely pitying and feeling sorry for people and start treating them as our allies in changing our society.

Our second task as Christian women is to struggle for women's right to jobs that have often been reserved for men. Training is demanded here. As women, we have the potential to be trained for the worthwhile jobs that are often assigned only to men.

A third task is for us to work for the banning of prostitution. Prostitution should be treated as illegal. What is really surprising is that prostitution is supposed to be illegal in our country but nobody is objecting to it. In Manila, we have 24- hour duty people who help treat venereal diseases in the prostitution district.

What can be done to really solve this problem? Women should start getting the cooperation of men to help solve the problem—men who are somehow grateful to God for their mothers, sisters and their wives and would want to join us in the effort. We will be laughed at, we will be marked and there would be all sorts of hindrances in trying to ban prostitution. The opposition will come from both prostitutes and prostitute users, such as the military. It is so sad that it is assumed that if you want to satisfy soldiers then you have to provide them with women. So that is how the issues of military bases are always connected to the issue of prostitution. Why can we not be more creative in providing soldiers with more wholesome recreation? Why can we not help humanize them? Why is it that it is assumed that this is a need that should be provided for? Is there no way out?

Then of course, there remains the fourth task of the serious rehabilitation of prostitutes. This is a delicate thing. As I said before, they should not feel that we regard them as those who have "dirtied" or degraded themselves. They themselves would tell us of their real need for a new life.

My final remark is a reminder for all of us who are not of the poor class that we need to address the issue of poverty, if we are to take the issue of prostitution seriously. Why is it that there are human beings who cannot have their basic needs met? What is wrong with our economic, political structures? What is wrong with our community life? All this is a big issue and we could immediately be branded as Marxist, communist or what have you if we stubbornly insist on dealing with the issue of poverty and putting it in the forefront. For as someone said, "when I gave something to the poor I was called a saint, but when I asked WHY there are the poor I was called a communist."

The issue of poverty is a complicated one. But are we, women, really willing to be part of the group that would address the issue? How can the issue of poverty be addressed effectively? For this is at the root of prostitution, at the root of the degradation of persons, especially of women!

I hope that we will seriously consider the tasks before us. I also hope that what I have shared today will challenge us to reread Scriptures through the eyes of women.

8

The Emergence of Asian Feminist Consciousness of Culture and Theology

Kwok Pui-lan (Hong Kong)

Theological reflection on the dynamic relation between culture and theology is of crucial importance in constructing Asian women's theology. Virginia Fabella, a Maryknoll sister from the Philippines, has aptly stated:

> What distinguishes Asia from the rest of the Third World is its religious, cultural, and linguistic pluralism. Asia has at least seven major linguistic zones, more than any other continent can claim. It is the birthplace of all the great world religions and, with the exception of Christianity and Judaism, it is the home of most of their adherents.[1]

Asian Christian women, as a tiny minority in Asian societies, have to struggle to live out both our identities as Asian and as Christian among our people, most of whom do not share our religious faith. The theological issue of how to relate Christianity to Asian cultural and religious traditions needs to be clarified, lest we will live in constant tension or even in schizophrenia. Furthermore, it needs to be examined from both the female and male perspectives because Christian faith and Asian traditions affect women and men differently.

I would attempt to outline here the emergence of Asian feminist consciousness of culture and theology from a historical perspective. The discussion is based on my ongoing research on Chinese women and Christianity, and many conversations with Asian sisters in the ecumenical movement. At the outset, I would like to stress that the following account represents only one way to look at the complex issue, as there are many different approaches to interpret our heritages and histories. It is written as a sincere and open invitation to engage more people in the continuing dialogue. The discussion will be divided into three parts. Part one examines the emergence of critical feminist consciousness in the nineteenth century, a period when Asian churches were heavily dominated by missionary influences. Part two brings us into the twentieth century when Asian women began to reassess Christianity in the context of rising nationalism and people's aspiration for independence. The concluding part discusses issues raised by Asian women theologians when we construct Asian theology, taking serious consideration of our identities as Asians and women.

MISSION, CHURCH, AND CULTURAL ICONOCLASM

Christianity was brought into encounter with Asian culture through the missionary movement. Many Asian churches were formed as a direct result of missionary activities by European and American mission boards during the nineteenth century, which has often been referred to as the "great century of Christian mission." The magnitude of missionary activities can be illustrated by the example of China, one of the biggest mission fields. In 1907, when the Chinese Church celebrated the centenary of Protestant missions in China, there were 3,745 foreign missionaries, representing more than 60 mission bodies.[2]

It is important to examine more closely the relation between mission, culture, and Christianity from the women's perspective. The nineteenth century missionary movement can be attributed to evangelical revivalism on both sides of the Atlantic, as well as to military and political expansion of the West. Missionaries, with an evangelical zeal, went to Third World countries to preach the Gospel to the "heathen," whom they considered to be living in the dark without the Gospel of Jesus. Although some of these missionaries attempted to learn the native language and mix with the people, the majority of them demonstrated a kind of ethnocentrism, believing that their own culture and religion were unmistakably superior. Such biased attitudes were further reinforced by an evolutionary view in the study of world religions current at that time, which saw "the history of religion as a process of progressive development of evolution in which ever higher and purer forms emerge."[3] Christianity was presumed to be the highest stage of development or the ultimate fulfillment of all religions.

The cultural imperialistic presuppositions of the missionaries were criticized by both Asian Christians and conscientious scholars in the West.[4] Asian Christian women must also reassess our past to see what we can learn from history, because the missionary movement has seldom been evaluated from women's view point. In fact, the lives and work of Asian Christian women and female missionaries have just begun to receive serious attention by scholars.[5] Women's mission boards mushroomed both in Europe and America in the latter half of the nineteenth century. The journals of these women's boards often portrayed women of the Third World as pitiful, secluded, and illiterate to generate support for missionary activities. Oppression of women in non-Western societies was dramatically depicted both as a symbol of the inferiority of their culture and as justification for sending women missionaries. In contrast, Christianity was seen as uplifting for women, and to

Christianize "heathen mothers" was deemed as the undeniable "white women's burden."

Owing to the patriarchal church structure, women missionaries were not sent as priests, but as educators, evangelists, social workers, and doctors, working chiefly among women and children. Their daily exposures to some of the oppression Asian women faced, such as arranged marriage, bonded labour, and female infanticide, made them more aware of their own subordination and the harmful effects of sexual exploitation. In colonial and semi-colonial Asian countries, these women missionaries enjoyed unexpected feminine power, which they were denied back in their own countries. Some of them took as their task providing female education and improving the plight of women. The first girls' school in Asia was opened by missionaries in Sri Lanka, and mission schools for girls were subsequently founded in many other countries.[6]

While we should not condone ethnocentrism in women's missionary literature and the condescending attitude exhibited by some of the women missionaries, we need to point out that the "feminization of the mission force" resulted in greater attention paid to women's issues. Furthermore, the tiny Christian churches, existing as marginal groups in Asian societies, provided an alternative to the dominant patriarchal culture and social relationships.[7] Christian churches attracted women because they allowed them to step outside familial roles to explore new possibilities. Women could learn to read, sing songs, enjoy fellowship, and exercise some form of religious leadership in their local religious communities. Some women were inspired by the gospel message which spoke of Jesus as compassionate to women, recognizing their worth as human beings.

Christianity, as a foreign religion, had the iconoclastic effect of opening Asian women's eyes to deep-seated patriarchal traditions embedded in their own culture. By presenting a radically different world view and a new set of rituals, Christianity helped to liberate our Christian foremothers from a kind of cultural anesthesia to question the legitimacy of those social and religious institutions which kept women in their inferior place. In the late nineteenth century, Christian women in China began to challenge the thousand-year-old tradition of foot-binding. In many parts of Asia, Christian women refused to adhere to the traditional marriage and funeral ceremonies which undergirded the patriarchal and patrilineal family system. Hundreds and thousands of women and girls started going to school, defying the social norm that women's place should be in the kitchen.

In their own ways, our foremothers had begun to look at their own culture *as women*, which was the first step towards the development of critical feminist consciousness. The Christian community, serving as an institutional base for sisterhood and fellowship, also provided the context for organized action against oppressive structures in the society. The Woman's Christian Temperance Movement, the Y.W.C.A., the Woman's Clubs were formed to raise women's consciousness, provide Christian service for women and children, and effect changes in social morality. When we study our own church history in the misssionary period, it seems that we have too often concentrated on what the missionaries had done or had not done. It is time for Asian Christian women to reclaim our history and to underscore the emergence of critical feminist consciousness as our important legacy.

NATIONALISM AND A CRITIQUE OF CHRISTIANITY

The turn of the century saw the rising aspirations of Asian people for national independence and self autonomy. For example, Filipino people struggled to overthrow Spanish colonialism in the independence movement of 1898, and Koreans had striven for political autonomy ever since it was colonized by Japan in 1895. In China, the early twentieth century marked the end of the millenia-old monarchy and the struggle for freedom from foreign encroachment. Women and men, young and old, shed their blood, laying down their lives for freedom, human dignity, and national integrity. Students, workers, and intellectuals joined hand-in-hand in demonstrations and people's movements for the liberation of their motherland from the yoke of colonialism and military aggression.

The fundamental challenge of national salvation made Asian women more conscious of their responsibility toward society and the bondage of patriarchy which weakened the nation by excluding the contribution of one-half of the people. Participation in revolutionary and political activities enabled women to explore new roles traditionally denied them.[8] In some Asian countries, such as Korea and China, women began publishing their own journals, propagating the ideas of sexual equality, human rights of women, and a new social order.[9] Asian women writers reported and discussed feminist activities in the West, such as the struggle for universal suffrage and economic opportunities, encouraging female readers to stand up for their own rights.

Women's rising consciousness in Asia provided the critical context for Christian women to articulate and challenge the patriarchal traditions and practices of the Church. While women were demonstrating and fighting for sexual equality in society, Christian women were alert to the injustices existing in the Christian community, for example, women could not preach from the pulpit and were not accepted to the Holy Order. The same Christian community, which was prophetic in terms of women's emancipation in the nineteenth century, seemed to be caught up by traditional patriarchal ecclesiologies, failing to catch up with the changing circumstances of the time.

The critique of Christianity, however, did not come from women alone, but also from other Asian intellectuals who began to see the subtle and intricate links between the missionary enterprise and military and political expansion of the West. In China, for example, radical intellectuals in the 1920's attacked Christianity as superstitious and as handmaiden of foreign aggression. Marxist theory, which was introduced to China in the late 1910's, offered a ready- made theoretical framework to evaluate Christianity's role in the imperialistic era. College students and university professors joined together in the Anti-Christian Movement of 1922-1927, condemning activities of the

Christian Church and demanding educational autonomy from the control of missions.[10] Interestingly, one of the criticisms levelled against Christianity was its oppression of women. The Creation story was charged as justifying women's subordination and the patriarchal church structure was condemned as oppressive.[11]

In China as in other Asian countries, more and more Christian women recognise that church teachings inherited from the missionary movement are not fitting both from the point of women and from the point of Asian people's struggle for liberation. Asian Christian women in the early twentieth century began a self-conscious effort to re-examine the Bible and delineate the liberating motifs in the Christian tradition. They emphasized that women and men are created in the image of God, Jesus treats women fairly and with compassion, and the Apostle Paul states that there is neither male nor female in Christ. Others raised the hermeneutical issue whether the patriarchal prescriptions of the Bible could be unconditionally applied to the Asian context without qualifications.[12] These writings by Christian women, scattered in small pamphlets, church newspapers, religious journals, and women's publications must be gathered and treasured by us as alternative resources for doing theology from women's perspective.

RECLAIMING THE PAST, CHARTING THE FUTURE

In the past decade, something exciting and new has been happening among Asian Christian women, that is, we have begun to enter into ecumenical dialogue with one another. In ecumenical conferences and forums, we meet one another face to face, compare our notes and listen to each other's personal testimony. We cry with pain for the continued oppressions of Asian women and rejoice that our passion for justice and peace unites us despite our cultural and linguistic differences. Learning to value each other's writings, we patiently struggle through the foreign words (often in transliteration), listening with open hearts to the mourning and yearning underlying the written text. Our ecumenical encounters prompt us to take our Asian identity with utmost seriousness and deepen our commitment to the future destiny of Asian people.[13]

Contemporary Asian women theologians continue the cultural critique our foremothers have begun, pointing out that the patriarchal Asian traditions, such as Confucianism, Hinduism, and Buddhism still exert tremendous influences on women's lives. However, most of the criticisms are based on the patriarchal teachings and motifs in the ancient Asian classic texts, without looking at how these traditions actually function to oppress women in the historical context. The important work of Elisabeth Schüssler Fiorenza has cautioned us that the written text may not represent the actual experiences of women, and we must "move from androcentric texts to their social-historical contexts."[14] Women were not simply victims in the patriarchal culture. We have to examine how they coped and negotiated with, as well as resisted the patriarchal culture. Scholars in the study of religion also point out that even in patriarchal religions such as Hinduism and Christianity, women formed their own religious communities, developed their rituals and celebrated their own festivals.

Although I have grown up in the Confucian tradition which has been criticized by Koreans, Chinese, and Japanese for its patriarchal teachings, I am not convinced that I have to discard it completely. Current interest in Confucianism both in China and in international circles has opened up new horizons to look at this tradition. Scholars no longer look at Confucianism just as a powerful ideology which was used to oppress the masses, including women, but also as a religio-philosophy offering inspiring symbolic resources for understanding what is fully human.[15] Moreover, Confucianism is not the sole tradition that informs the religiosity of East Asian people because of the co-existence of religious Taoism, folk Buddhism, and other popular religions. The dynamic interaction between these different traditions needs to be further clarified from women's point of view. For example, recent excavations in the northeastern part of China indicate there was once the worship of female figurines and mother earth around 5000 B.C.[16] How did this earlier stratum of goddess-worship relate to later development of Confucianism? In East Asian countries, Taoism, which uses female imagery in the classical texts and allows women to serve as priests, co-existed with the predominant Confucian tradition. How the two competed for orthodoxy and for followers is another relevant issue for women.

Besides criticizing patriarchal traditions, Asian women theologians also look into alternative resources to construct their theology, especially those repressed elements that have been labelled as "dangerous," or "unimportant." For example, Korean women are re-examining the songs and dances in shamanism, a popular religious tradition in which women often play significant symbolic and ritualistic roles. Indian women are looking at their invaluable treasures of folk-literature and the long tradition of goddess-worship to discern their significance for today.[17] Filipino women unravel layers of colonial traditions to examine the myths and legends before the Spanish conquest.[18]

Our serious digging into women's historical, cultural, and religious resources opens our eyes to the treasures that have hitherto been unexplored by Asian theologians. We have come to a new appraisal of women's tradition in Asia when we begin to raise questions from a feminist perspective. For example, I have long assumed that the Goddess of Mercy (*Guanyin* in Chinese, *Kannon* in Japanese) has functioned to reinforce the patriarchal family system because the Goddess was believed to be able to bestow women with a son. It was only after I had done some research on this religious symbol that I became aware that in the original Chinese legend, the Goddess was a courageous woman who defied her father's will by refusing to enter into an arranged marriage.[19] Since then, I have paid more attention to women's religious experiences when they worship the Goddess, instead of simply listening to what the dominant culture has interpreted for us.

Stretching our theological imagination, our critique and rediscovery of our past traditions raises the question of adequacy of the theological model we have inherited. For example, we begin to ask questions such as: How to integrate and synthesize what we have learnt from our cultural contexts with theological reflection? How can we enter into meaningful dialogue with Asian sisters of other religious faiths? What are the norms to select our cultural resources and what kind of hermeneutical principle is appropriate to interpret them? In a nutshell, we have to develop our own theology of culture.

In the sixties, Asian theologians used the paradigm of "inculturation," "indigenization," or "accommodation" to speak of the process of re-rooting Christianity into Asia soil.[20] Although these words might have slightly different meanings, they basically connote that there is a body of theological truths to be "adapted," or "accommodated" to the Asian context. Today, Asian women theologians must point out the limitations of such an approach. First, it takes the content of the Bible and the Gospel for granted, without seriously challenging the androcentric bias both in the biblical texts and in the core symbolism of Christianity. Secondly, it identifies with Asian culture too readily, often failing to see that many Asian traditions are overtly patriarchal.

In the past several years, a new paradigm has emerged as more Asian theologians are committed to do theology with Asian resources. It is more constructive and imaginative because this time we start not from Western theology and foreign concepts, but from local and indigenous resources, folk-literature, people's history, and religious texts. C.S. Song has said, "Doing theology in Asia today is exciting because it is no longer dictated by rules and norms established elsewhere outside our living space called Asia. Its contents are not determined any more by schools and systems of theology formed under the influence of cultural elements alien to cultural experiences of Asia. Its styles—yes, one must speak of style of doing theology—does not have to be shaped by thought-forms and life-experiences remote from Asian humanity."[21]

This approach may be more promising for Asian women's theology since it encourages us to probe into a new arena and experiment with innovative styles of doing theology. For example, we must allow the possibility of doing theology in poems, songs, stories, dances, rituals, and even lullabies. But we must insist that women's resources must be treated with equal attention, and the new theological style must reflect both male and female experiences. Secondly, the feminist critique of culture and theology, which is an important legacy from our foremothers, must be one of the most significant norms in selecting and appropriating Asian resources. Thirdly, the challenge of Asian women's theology is nothing less than the reformulation of some basic elements of Christian theology and ethics such as the relations between divine and human, monotheism and plurality of religious symbolism, between cosmological vision and social action, and between male and female in the context of the international flesh trade and sex tourism.

Remembering the past, Asian Christian women gain fresh insight into the power of history in shaping hope. Encouraged by the daring examples of our foremothers, we are more committed to the struggle for justice and sexual equality of humankind. As we embark onto a journey full of risks and possibilities, we have to create our road along the way. Our hearts are warmed by the ecumenical fellowship of women and men who are also earnestly seeking God's Kingdom on earth. Together with Third World sisters, we are developing a new way of doing theology, which not only liberates us, but the generations to come.

NOTES

1. Virginia Fabella, "A Common Methodology for Diverse Christologies," in *With Passion and Compassion: Third World Women Doing Theology,* ed., Virgina Fabella and Mercy Amba Oduyoye (Maryknoll, New York: Orbis Books, 1988), 109.

2. *China Centenary Missionary Conference Records* (New York: American Tract Society, n.d.), 782.

3. Owen C. Thomas, ed., *Attitudes toward Other Religions* (London: SCM, 1969), 22.

4. For example C.S. Song, *Christian Mission in Reconstruction—An Asian Attempt* (Madras: Christian Literature Society, 1975); and William R. Hutchison, *Errand to the World: American Protestant Thought and Foreign Mission* (Chicago: University of Chicago Press, 1987).

5. For example Jane Hunter, *The Gospel of Gentility: American Women Missionaries in the Turn-of-the-century China* (New Haven: Yale University Press, 1984); and Patricia R. Hill, *The World Their Household: The American Woman's Foreign Mission Movement and Cultural Transformation,* 1870-1920 (Ann Arbor: The University of Michigan Press, 1985). I am completing a doctoral dissertation on "Chinese Women and Christianity 1860-1927" at Harvard Divinity School.

6. This information was provided by Anita Neshiah of Sri Lanka during a conversation in Boston, 1987.

7. For the Chinese situation, see Daniel H. Bays, "Christianity and the Chinese Sectarian Tradition," *Ch'ing-shih Wen-ti* (Issues in Qing history) 4/7 (1982): 35-55; for the Japanese situation, see Yasuko Morihara Grosjean, "The 'Silent Victims' Speak," *Journal of Feminist Studies in Religion* 3/2 (1987): 108-109.

8. See Maita Gomez, "Women's Organizations as Offshoots of National, Political Movements," in *Essays on Women,* ed. Mary John Mananzan (Manila: St. Scholastica's College, 1987), 54.

9. See Sung-Hee Lee, "Women's Liberation Theology as the Foundation for Asian Theology," *East Asia Journal of Theology* 4/2 (1986): 9-10; and Charlotte L. Beahan, "Feminism and Nationalism in the Chinese Women's Press, 1902-1922," *Modern China* 1 (1975): 379-416.

10. Alice H. Gregg, *China and Educational Autonomy* (New York: Syracuse University Press, 1946), 101-142.

11. See C.S. Chang, *Guonei jin shinian lai zongjiao sichao* (Religious thought movements in China during the last decade) (Beijing: Yenching School of Chinese Studies, 1927), 239; and Jinzhang Pang, "Jidujiao shi mieshi nuxing mo?" (Does Christianity despise women?) *Zhenli Zhoukan* (Truth Weekly) 42 (January 13, 1924): 1.

12. See my other article, "Mothers and Daughters, Writers and Fighters," in *Inheriting Our Mothers' Gardens: Feminist Theology in Third World Perspective* (Philadelphia: The Westminster Press, 1988), 26-29.

13. See Sun Ai Lee Park, "Asian Women's Theological Reflection," *East Asia Journal of Theology* 3/2 (1985): 172-182.

14. Elisabeth Schussler Fiorenza, *In Memory of Her: A Feminist Theological Reconstruction of Christian Origins* (New York: Crossroad, 1983), 29.

15. Refer to the important works of Tu Wei-ming, especially his *Confucian Thought: Selfhood as Creative Transformation* (New York: State University of New York, 1985).

16. Guo Daishun,"Liaoning sheng kezuo yuan dongshanju hongshan wenhua jian-zhu qunzhi fajue jianbao" (Report on excavations in Liaoning Province) *Wenwu* (November 1984), 1-11.

17. The Asian Women's Resource Centre for Culture and Theology convened a consultation on Goddesses and Asian women theology in the fall of 1988. The papers will be published in a forthcoming issue of *In God's Image*. This quarterly journal is available by writing to the Asian Women's Resource Centre at 566 Nathan Road, Kiu Kin Mansion, 6th floor, Kowloon, Hong Kong.

18. Mary John Mananzan, "The Filipino Woman: Before and After the Spanish Conquest of the Philippines," in *Essays on Women,* 7-36.

19. P. Steven Sangren, "Female Gender in Chinese Religious Symbols: Kuan Yin, Ma Tsu and the 'Eternal Mother'." *Signs* 9 (1981): 7.

20. For example Kosuke Koyama, *Theology in Contact* (Madras: Christian Literature Society, 1975), 54-69; and Aloysius Chang, "The Inculturation of Theology in the Chinese Church," *Gregorianum* 63/1 (1982): 5-59.

21. C.S. Song,"Let us Do Theology with Asian Resources!" *East Asia Journal of Theology* 3/2 (1985): 207-208.

9

Redefining Religious Commitment in the Philippine Context

Mary John Mananzan (Philippines)

To be a Christian today in a land where injustice and oppression abide is a challenge. To be a woman religious in such a situation is doubly so. It calls for a radical re-thinking of the meaning of being a Christian and of the imperative of religious commitment. It precipitates a spiritual crisis. It demands a consequent revision of one's way of life—a true conversion, a *metanoia.*

This paper will not be a theoretical speculation of what could be the challenges of being a woman religious today, but is a sharing of actual experiences and ongoing reflection on them. Some of these reflections have already been put in writing so I will quote extensively from my own articles.

SOCIETAL CONTEXT AND PERSONAL COMMITMENT

One of the most valuable insights of liberation theology is the contextualization of theological reflection and the necessity of the analysis of society as its starting point. It is likewise the characteristic of this way of theologizing to regard one's involvement in the process of societal liberation as the substance of its reflection. This first section will therefore be devoted to these two important points.

Characteristics of Philippine Society

I am a woman religious living in a Third World country, the Philippines. My country is known as the only Christian country in the Far East, having been christianized by the Spanish colonization in the sixteenth century. It remained a Spanish colony for roughly three and a half centuries and then fell into the hands of the United States in 1898, becoming its colony for the next fifty years. It was occupied by the Japanese for three years during the Second World War. It became independent in 1946 and was put under martial law in 1972, suffering twenty years of one-man rule which ended in the famous EDSA event of February 1986.

But this event, impressive as it was, did not end the misery of the people. There was a change in the head of the nation but there was no change in the class of those who rule. The oppressive political machinery and its armed component remains. The orientation of the country's economic development model continues. In other words, there was no social revolution. Thus the fundamental problems of the people still prevail—namely, the grossly inequitable distribution of resources (2 percent of its 56 million inhabitants owning and controlling 75 percent of land and capital); and the foreign control of its economy through transnational corporations and through the debt link to the IMF and World Bank. U.S. interventions into its economic and political life have in fact become more overt. These core problems have been responsible for the massive poverty with dire consequences such as malnourished and brain damaged children, unemployment and underemployment, brain and muscle drain, chronic insurgency and intensifying militarization that has cost so many Filipino lives.

Baptism of Fire

It was the same situation of crisis, oppression, and injustice that made me respond to a telephone brigade in 1975 asking nuns, seminarians, and priests to come to the rescue of six hundred striking workers in a wine factory, La Tondena. It was the first strike attempted after the strike ban issued following the declaration of martial law in September 1972.

I had just come from a six-year study leave in Germany and Rome, and I was teaching contemporary philosophy in a Jesuit University. I joined a group called "Interfaith Theological Circle," which aimed at evolving a "Filipino Theology" in the air-conditioned library of the university. Needless to say we came under critique for doing "intellectual gymnastics" in spite of producing what appeared to us as extremely erudite papers on the subject. After a period of defensiveness, we realized that it was indeed futile to evolve such a theology without getting involved in the struggle of the people. This was what made me respond to the invitation of the La Tondena workers. There I had my first encounter with military brutality and experienced helplessness before the reality of force and institutional violence. That was where we established the "Friends of the Workers."

The La Tondena strike inspired a hundred more strikes in a period of three months as we went from one factory to the other, gaining valuable learning experiences from the people, getting an insight into the root causes of their problems. Helping workers immersed us in the problems of slum dwellers, for the workers lived in slums. We joined human barricades to stop demolitions. We formed groups that spearheaded rallies and marches. We were recruited into negotiating teams to face the military in mass actions. And inevitably we got involved in the fate of political detainees who were arrested in marches, rallies, and pickets and snatched from their houses in midnight raids.

The Anguish of Awareness

This initiation into the struggles of the people shook the framework of my Christian and religious existence. I quote at length an article I wrote at the time describing this experience:

> Social awareness can mean real anguish. Exposures even on a minor scale to the miseries of our people and a serious reflection on these experiences can confront us with facts that would question our former values. And yet it takes time to adopt and synthesize a new set of values one is beginning to perceive. One is back to zero during this period. One is barren. One stops giving talks or writing articles, because one feels empty, one needs to be reeducated. This awareness gives one a sense of urgency that may seem fanatic to those who either do not see or who confine social consciousness to community assemblies. Here is where one can make a mistake in strategy, become overzealous, and turn off people. But there is indeed a constriction of the heart, which one feels when one talks with persons who see no further than the four protective walls of their houses or convents. Here is where awareness can cause real loneliness. All of a sudden one is on a different plane when talking with one's family, one's closest friends and colleagues. Not to be able to share values can be a painful form of isolation and the slow, painstaking trial and error attempts to share these new values and new imperatives without turning people off can bring one to a point of helplessness and frustration further aggravated by one's clearer and closer perception of the magnitude of the problem and the uncertainty, risks, and corresponding magnitude of the proposed solutions. To confront in others time and time again one's own prejudice, one's own blind spots, one's own doubts, is to relive time and time again one's own *metanoia* without the sense of relief at the thought that the decision and choice lies within one's power. But perhaps the greatest anguish is the yawning gap between one's insight and one's generosity. Insight brings with it imperatives to action that may mean crucial decisions, and to perceive and yet not to have the courage or moral energy to act is a real agony. To conscientize is truly a serious business, because the price of awareness is anguish.[1]

To take stock of things and to understand what was happening to themselves, thirty priests and sisters initiated an alternative retreat, which they called *Hakbang* (step forward). These were five days of sharing in-depth experiences of how they got involved, a sharing of anxieties, doubts, apprehensions, fears, hopes, engaging in an analysis both of the society and the church, and formulating visions for both a transformed society and a renewed church. Everyday was climaxed by a creative liturgy that recapitulated the sharing during the day. This alternative retreat was repeated for other groups. The result was a leveling of consciousness, a greater clarity of vision, a renewed courage born out of common experiences of personal liberation, and a greater motivation to go forward.

Intensified Involvement in the Struggle of the Oppressed

One important insight that emerged from the Hakbang was the need to analyze reality and a greater systematization of commitment. Tools of analysis were learned, adapted, systematized, applied, and shared. Focusing of one's energies brought about a sort of division of labor.

I became chairperson of the Task Force Orientation of Church Personnel of the Association of Major Religious Superiors in the Philippines. My team and I designed modules for conscientization seminars which we gave to religious, priests, teachers, school administrators, and church workers all over the country and even at times to certain other parts of Asia. The modules consisted of a biblical perspective, church history, analysis of society, institutional analysis (of religious congregations, schools, or groups), formulation of common thrusts, and systematic planning. We likewise organized rank- and -file sisters into the National Organization of Religious Women in the Philippines (NOW-RP).

As dean of college of a school for women, I worked out with my faculty a reorientation of the school toward an education for social transformation. We revised the school's mission statement, its objectives as well as those of the different departments. A Third World perspective was adopted in the revision of the curriculum. We formed a team to give conscientization seminars to both the faculty and students. Later on the cocurricular activities were likewise reoriented. Behavioral objectives for the kind of students we wanted to educate were formulated. Criteria for evaluation of what a socially-oriented school should concretely manifest were likewise clearly described. Innovative methods such as exposure programs, panel discussions with grassroot leaders, tent fora, discussion groups, and the like were devised. Administration, faculty, and students met each other at rallies, demonstrations, pickets, and other forms of mass actions. Themes on different aspects of an education for justice were focused on each year: social awareness, commitment, involvement, community building. Periodic evaluation and departmental audits were made to ensure understanding and implementation of the orientation. Through years of trial and error, small advances and setbacks, an outside accrediting team could write in 1987, twelve years after the reorientation was launched, the following observation:

> One very prominent characteristic of the school is the stress on Christian commitment manifesting itself in social justice and social responsibility especially toward the poor, the marginalized, and the oppressed. This feature is visible not only in the activities especially oriented toward community involvement. It seems to pervade the whole atmosphere and

life of the school.[2]

In 1978, when a series of oil price hikes was decided without consultation of the people, a group of twelve persons founded the Citizens' Alliance for Consumer Protection, of which I became the secretary general up to this day. This organization tackled consumer issues, such as price hikes, junk foods, banned drugs, breastfeeding, nuclear energy, fertilizers and pesticides, taxes, in the context of the national economy. It grew into a federation of organizations that could mobilize rallies, demonstrations, boycotts, and marches. It launched consumer education through lectures, seminars, radio programs, and a mobile theater.

The energy desk of this association was formed when the government of President Marcos started to resist the Bataan Nuclear Free Philippines Coalition. This and other antinuclear organizations such as NO NUKES succeeded in putting a stop to the nuclear plant. They also successfully lobbied for a nuclear-weapons-free provision in the constitution and are at present lobbying for the removal of the U.S. bases in the Philippines.

Commitment to Women's Concerns

The feminist movement is new in the Philippines. Although concerned with prostitution in the Philippines, I did not get involved in the feminist movement until 1978 when I was invited to a World Council of Churches Conference in Venice on human rights and women. When I returned to the Philippines I cofounded with three other women the *Filipina*, which can be considered the first organization of women with a conscious and expressedly feminist orientation. With another woman I established the Center for Women Resources. This latter took the initiative in 1984 to call a conference of all women's organizations that mushroomed at the time. In this conference, the federation of women's organizations, GABRIELA, was born. It is now the most extensive federation of women in the Philippines, counting a hundred organizations and about 40,000 individual members. In 1986 I was elected its national chairperson and in 1987 reelected for a period of two years.

GABRIELA has clearly defined the orientation of the women's movement in a Third World country like the Philippines. It sees women's liberation within the context of the economic, political, and cultural transformation of society. This is the necessary though not sufficient condition of women's liberation. There is no total human liberation without the liberation of women in society. And this is not an automatic consequence of either economic development or political revolution. In other words, the women's movement is an essential aspect of the very process of societal liberation.

GABRIELA makes use of seven main strategies to achieve its goal. The most important strategy is organization, because oppressed groups are empowered by organization. GABRIELA is organized according to sectors, regions, and areas of interest. GABRIELA members are mobilized along national issues, such as foreign bases, foreign debts, consumer issues. It also initiates campaigns on specifically women's concerns such as prostitution, mail-order brides and domestic violence. The third strategy is education, both formal and informal, institutional and noninstitutional. It is of utmost importance to awaken the awareness of women to their situation because the great majority of them have internalized their oppression. The fourth strategy, feminist scholarship differs from education by its emphasis on the development of the women's perspective in the different academic disciplines—for example, psychology, history. The legal strategy achieved a major victory when the women's campaign on women's rights resulted in the inclusion of the equal rights provision in the newly ratified Philippine Constitution. For women who are victims of violence, crisis centers are being established for legal, medical, and psychological aid. The urban poor women in slum areas have been helped by livelihood projects, day care centers, and primary health care clinics. These constitute the welfare strategy. Finally, the women believe in an international solidarity strategy because the women's cause is a universal cause. Every year the international desk of GABRIELA organizes a WISAP (Women International Solidarity Affair Philippines) conference attended by women from different parts of the world.

The Cost of Commitment

In the preceding pages, the anguish of awareness has been shared. This is preliminary to the cost of commitment. In the thirteen years that I have been involved in the struggle of the poor and the oppressed in the Philippines, I have witnessed tremendous costs of commitment of persons I knew and worked with, ranging from black propaganda, disappearances, arbitrary arrests, torture, political detention and rape, to massacre, assassinations, and "salvaging."

I have been labeled a "communist" subversive and have been served a subpoena for speaking at a rally on the oil price hike, which was considered "agitation for rebellion." Not only is one harassed by the military and by the conservative press, one is likewise subject to the suspicions of church officials who feel "disturbed" and "threatened." There is also the alienation of former friends and relatives who cannot understand one's commitment and involvement.

THEOLOGICAL REFLECTION

With a group of theologically trained persons called THRUST[3] and a wider interdisciplinary group called FIDES,[4] theological reflection on the continuous struggle is being undertaken. Lately, the group has published its first volume, *Religion and Society: Towards a Theology of Struggle*. I would like to discuss this work by sharing our efforts and insights in three ongoing endeavors: reflecting on a theology of struggle, developing a feminist theology of liberation in Asia, and evolving a new spirituality.

It was only after years of being involved in the struggle that the groups who hesitated to put down anything in writing, because it seemed difficult to write something while one is still undergoing a process, decided to make tentative written reflections about what they were experiencing. The term "theology of struggle" emerged from these reflections although there was no claim of forming a theological school. As Fely Carino puts it: "There were no pretensions here of making or developing a new dogmatic theology or of laying claim to a new theological discovery that could be included in the ever-expanding index of theological constructs." Rather,

> what was foremost in their minds and what was the focus of their atten-
> tion was the sharpening of the Philippine struggle itself and how Chris-
> tians can participate and contribute fully in that struggle. More impor-
> tant to these are questions of equipment and empowerment, and the
> usefulness and serviceability of the Christian tradition in theological,
> liturgical, and symbolic expression to make Christians more effective in
> the struggle to bring about transformed Philippine society and an equally
> transformed Philippine church.[5]

It is therefore clear that this theology is not about "struggle," but it is first and foremost theology "in" and "of" the struggle.

One of the first exponents of this theologizing is Carlos Abesamis, SJ. His scriptural work of twenty-five years has provided it with a biblical perspective. Fr. Abesamis, using the creedal statement of the Bible, has developed a theology of total and concrete salvation, which traces this concept through the different periods of the Old and New Testaments and of the early church. Salvation, as experienced by our foreparents of the faith, Abesamis writes, "was not salvation of the soul from sin but the bestowing of the blessing that affects the totality of life of an Israelite and of the Israelitic nation."[6] It is total because it affects the whole person, not only the soul, and also because it is not only for the individual but for society as a whole. It is concrete because it is a liberation from concrete evils such as poverty, slavery, injustice, oppression, sin; and because it means the working out of concrete blessings, which, though these cannot be perfected in this world, begin here and now.

On this biblical foundation I built my own reflections on church history. The dichotomies of matter/spirit, heaven/earth, body/soul came into Christianity not from its Hebrew tradition but from its hellenization. In an article entitled "The Religious Today and Integral Evangelization, " I explained:

> In its early years of growth, Christianity found itself flourishing in the
> Hellenistic culture of the Greco-Roman world. It is understandable that
> the early fathers of the church steeped in this culture explained and spread
> the teachings of Christianity in the conceptual framework in which they

found themselves. They use the categories of Greek philosophy, especially that of Plato, in their explanation and exposition of Christianity. It is not strange therefore that platonic dualism would now more and more influence Christian thought. Platonic dualism took three forms: *metaphysical*, the dualism of two worlds— the "real world" of ideas and the phenomenal world of senses; *epistemological*—the dualism of two forms of knowledge, the real innate knowledge of the world of ideas and opinion or sense knowledge; and the *psychological*— the dualism of body and soul.[7]

This accounted for the development of the other-worldly concept of salvation, its exclusive focus on the soul, and the suspicious outlook on the body and alienation from the world (*fuga mundi*). In the institutionalization of Christianity, systems of doctrine, morality and rituals were developed and were protected by a wall of orthodoxy. I realized the role of the "heretics" such as Galileo Galilei, Giordano Bruno, Meister Eckhart, and Teilhard de Chardin in the survival of the Church. They refused to be confined within the walls of orthodoxy and insisted at the cost of their reputation or even of their lives to rethink and rephrase theological concepts.

Vatican II made a breakthrough in tearing down the walls of orthodoxy and in the freer atmosphere of theological thought dichotomies were healed; the world began to be taken seriously as the only arena for salvation. This taking seriously of the world meant taking seriously its problems, the greatest of which is poverty. The Synod on Justice in 1972 added the insight that the deeper reality of poverty is injustice. Its document, *Justice in the World,* made the programmatic statement in the Introduction: "Action in behalf of justice and participation in the transformation of the world fully appears to us as a constitutive dimension of preaching the gospel."

This, I believe, formed the basis of all contextualized "theology of struggle" in the Philippine experience, because "justice" and "transformation of the world" would have remained abstract concepts if not taken in the concrete context of a particular place and time. The locus becomes the struggles for justice by oppressed peoples of particular countries in the world.

This change of theological perspective could not but exert an influence in the understanding of religious life. My own reflection on the matter appears in the same article cited previously. I wrote then:

> But even while turning her attention to these actions for justice, the religious has likewise to rethink her religious life, her vows, her spirituality, and lifestyle according to the insight that justice is a constituent dimension of her being a Christian and religious.
> The vow of poverty takes on more flesh and blood than the usual economizing or asking of permission. Poverty today must be truly experienced in the surrendering of vested interests, in true simple living, if possible, in "pitching one's tent" among the poor. At the very least

it would demand an unreserved sharing of one's resources with the poor and the oppressed.

Celibacy takes on a more positive meaning in the freedom of heart that is needed to be truly available to the many. Obedience can take on a new dimension in letting one's role be defined by the needs of the people. The *vox populi, vox Dei* adage takes on a new reality. One begins to listen with the ear of one's heart to people instead of dictating to them or taking the leading role. Just as there is a personal and communal poverty, there is likewise a personal and communal obedience. Congregations and religious communities have to learn to obey the signs of the times. They learn to insert themselves meaningfully into the local church where they find themselves.[8]

Developing an Asian Feminist Theology

As a *woman* religious, my commitment to the oppressed, which started with political militancy, developed into a commitment for the struggle of women against gender oppression. Again being a woman *religious* brought my attention to the religious roots of women's oppression. Together with Asian women coming from different religious and cultural backgrounds, we came to the insight that all religions have oppressive as well as liberating elements, which could serve for or against women; so far, more of the oppressive factors have been used to rationalize and justify the continued subordination of women.

The starting point of this Asian effort at theologizing from the women's perspective is the particular struggle of Asian women. The statement of the Asian Women's Consultation in Manila in November 1985 summarizes this in its first paragraph:

In all spheres of Asian society women are dominated, dehumanized, they are discriminated against, exploited, harassed, sexually used, abused, and regarded as inferior beings who must always subordinate themselves to the so-called male supremacy. In the home, church, education, and media, women have been treated with bias and condescension. In Asia and all over the world, the myth of the subservient, servile Asian woman is blatantly peddled to reenforce the dominant male stereotype image.[9]

The document then focused on the particular oppression of the different Asian women. Regarding Filipino women, it pinpoints the following oppressive factors:

Filipinas, like many of their Asian sisters, are subjected to job discrimination and are exposed to health hazards in factories, multinational companies, and export processing zones. Because of the severe economic crisis and with the advent of sex tourism and the presence of U.S. bases, many leave home to become migrant workers in hostile alien lands. Furthermore, many are raped, tortured, imprisoned, and killed for their political beliefs.[10]

This situation of Asian women was condemned as a "sinful situation."

An ecumenical group called AWIT (Association of Women in Theology) is engaged in reinterpreting biblical pericopes from the woman's point of view. The women realize that the Bible is often used to justify the subordination and discrimination of women, especially the creation story and the epistles of St. Paul. They denounce the misogynistic writings of the fathers and doctors of the church. They expose the introduction of the norms and practices of the patriarchal society in Philippine society. They criticize the domesticating role of theological concepts. Sr. Virginia Fabella, for example, makes the following critique of the way Mary has been taught and how the emerging feminist theology tries to correct it:

> One of the ways Catholicism has contributed to the subordination of women especially in the church, is by its portrayal of Mary. Through the ages Mary has been depicted as silent, sweet, self-effacing, docile, passive, submissive, a *Mater Dolorosa*. Actually this portrayal of Mary is a masculine perception of idealized femininity that has been inflicted on us and that many of us in turn have tried hard to internalize. In recent times, however, women have begun to appropriate the Bible for themselves without the mediation of male interpreters, and realize how Mary has been misrepresented. They see Mary of the gospel, especially of the Magnificat, as a woman of faith and intelligence, who is gentle and attentive, yet decisive and responsive, a woman of deep compassion but also of great courage, who is able to take the initiative and make great sacrifices and is willing to risk in order to accomplish God's word and will. This is, to a growing number of women, and should be to us, the true Mary, who is proto-disciple, yes, but above all, *woman*.[11]

Feminist liberation theology is still in its infancy in the Philippines and in Asia, but it has delineated for itself the following all-encompassing agenda:

> The agenda of renewal must include all aspects of theology from the reinterpretation of scriptures, to a historico-critical reflection of church doctrines from the women's point of view to the rediscovery of the great women of church history, to the fundamental questioning of the church's hierarchical structure, its constricting prescriptions, its discriminating practices, and the sexist language of its liturgy. It likewise includes the critical analysis of the particular culture in order to distinguish the liberative elements from oppressive forces that affect women.
> These will lead to the stripping away of the false consciousness of women and free her to discover herself and her potentialities and to come to

her full blossoming. In the running over of this bliss, she together with all peoples of God will use this energy toward the transformation of society into a "new heaven and a new earth."[12]

The Emerging Spirituality

Involvement in human struggles brings one to a spiritual crisis. I have described the anguish that comes with initial awareness and the costly consequences of commitment. One goes into a kind of dark night of the soul (*noche oscura*) and when one emerges, one experiences a shake-up in one's spirituality, which may result either in "giving up one's faith" (some of my friends have made this option) or one undergoes a real *metanoia*.

The emerging spirituality, in my experience, shows four trends. It is a spirituality that is liberational, integral, feminist, and oriental.

During the *Hakbang* or alternative retreat of the religious and priests mentioned in the beginning of this paper, each one shared his or her journey to commitment. The remarkable consensus was that each one experienced an inner liberation. Christ, the fully liberated person, became the inspiration. The involvement with oppressed persons helps one into a better self-knowledge and self-acceptance, which becomes the basis of an inner liberation manifesting itself in a growing freedom from fear, from idols, and from bitterness and resentment. Freedom from fear does not consist in not feeling fear but in the ability to distinguish between groundless fear and substantiated fear, and act in spite of such a substantiated fear. One becomes less worried about what the anonymous "they" might be thinking or criticizing. Besides being free from this "negative idol," one also experiences a freedom from legalism and from sacralizing law or from being enslaved to "positive idols" that one had put on pedestals during one's life. Although acknowledging the bitterness and resentment in one's negative experiences, one begins to transcend them into a creative and positive resolution of one's problems.

There is also a remarkable simplifying of one's faith and one's practices. There is an integration of the vertical and horizontal dimensions of one's religious life. To elaborate:

> It is understandable that one's spirituality will be influenced by this new thrust or else there will be a painful dichotomy. One's life of prayer will be "invaded" by the anguish of people. The psalms take on a relevance in confrontation with new pharaohs and a new Egypt or the need for a new Exodus and a new Promised Land. Liturgy will have to echo the crying aspirations of the oppressed as much as the joy of every step toward their liberation. The asceticism of the religious committed to justice need not be contrived. It will be imposed on her by the difficult situations that will inevitably arise; by the demands of people who cannot be put on a rigidly controlled timetable or calendar; by the expected persecution from the rich and powerful whose vested interests will be endangered; and by the misunderstandings of friends and loved ones who would be

threatened by one's radicality.[13]

The female perspective to spirituality developed as women started to reflect on their experiences as women, both personal and social, as well as on their common struggle against their manifold oppression. This spirituality is nourished by their growing understanding of their self-image which has been obscured by the roles that have been assigned to them by a patriarchal society. This in turn influences their interpersonal relationship and touches the collective consciousness that is growing among them as they struggle against exploitation and discrimination. It is shaped by the victories, small or big, which they have achieved in their struggle. Women's emerging spirituality is therefore not just a vertical relationship with God but an integral one. It is shaped not only by prayer but by relational experience and struggle, personal, interpersonal, and societal.

The release of creative energy and the new insights in the women's struggle have likewise affected a new focus and new expressions of spirituality. It is creation-centered rather than sin- and redemption-centered. It is holistic rather than dualistic. It is risk rather than security. It is a spirituality that is joyful rather than austere, active rather than passive, expansive rather than limiting. It celebrates more than it fasts; it lets go rather than holds back. It is an Easter rather than a Good Friday spirituality. It is vibrant, liberating, and colorful.

The holistic aspect that feminist influence has exerted on spirituality has likewise given rise to a phenomenon newly observed among activists in the Philippines, and that is the reclaiming of the contemplative heritage of Asia's great religions. More and more social activists in the Philippines are taking up the practice of Zen, which they undertake with great enthusiasm. Ruben Habito explains that the term "spirituality" equates with the Greek *pneuma* (spirit), which in turn equates with the Hebrew *ruah*, the breath of God. Throughout the Old and New Testaments, the breath of God plays a key role in all the events of salvation history from creation to the incarnation. Habito then shows the relationship between Zen practice and social militancy:

> Paying attention to one's breathing in Zen is seen not simply as a physical exercise that keeps one concentrated on one point, but as the very abandonment of one's total being to this Breath of God, here and now. It is letting one's whole self be possessed by the Spirit of God, to be vivified, guided, inspired, and fulfilled in it.
> And as one is "overshadowed" by the Spirit, one's whole being is offered for God's dynamic liberating action in history, to preach the good news to the poor. To proclaim release to the captives. To set at liberty those who are oppressed.[14]

In another way of expressing this, Sister Elaine MacInnes writes of the socially significant effect of Zen practice:

> Our dissipated energies gradually become more unified and we start to

112

gain some control over our superactive mind. Tensions are released, nerves are relaxed, and physical health generally improves. Emotions are sensitized. We begin to experience a kind of inner balance and gradually dryness, rigidity, hang-ups, prejudice, egoism melt and give way to compassion, serenity, egolessness, and social concern.[15]

The koan method presents the Zen student with "riddles," which the intellect will repel but which are grasped by the self-nature in an intuitive response. The student soon comes to see that everyday life is a koan which invites response. As Sister Elaine further writes: "when we see someone thirsty, we give a drink. When we are confronted with injustice, we cannot remain unmoved."[16]

This recourse to oriental mysticism for social activists closes the full circle of action/contemplative action.

CONCLUSION

Being a woman religious today is more difficult, less simple, more demanding, but definitely more challenging. When I hear a young woman answer the question "why do you want to enter the convent" with "because I want to have peace and quiet," I just smile.

The religious life has come a long way from the *fuga mundi* principle of the early days of monasticism. Women religious who were particularly the objects of enclosure laws of canon law because they were not only *religious* but *women,* have emerged from this constraint and have become involved in the burning issues of society and in some cases have been on the forefront of militant causes.

Personally, I find being a woman religious today in a Third World country a dangerous but challenging and meaningful existence. It forces one to go back to the original meaning of the core of the Christian message. Impelled by a sense of urgency because of the lived experience of suffering and oppression, women religious are inspired to a consequent living out of this Christian imperative in the concrete struggle of their world. This in turn gives them an experiential insight into the meaning of the paradox of committed freedom. The woman religious committed to justice becomes truly convinced that to seek her life is to lose it and to lose her life is to gain it, not only for herself but for others—for those who will perhaps see the fulfillment of her vision of a better world, something she will probably not see in her own lifetime.

NOTES

1. Mary John Mananzan, Editorial in *Conversatio*, September 1975.
2. Report of PAASCU Accrediting Team, August 1987, 1.
3. THRUST stands for Theologians for Renewal, Unity and Social Transforma-

tion. This is a group of concerned Christians doing theology from within the Church and actively participating in the struggle for full human liberation.

4. FIDES stand for Forum for Inter-Disciplinary Endeavors and Studies, a group of men and women of different professions, whose main task is the reformulation of a theology spirituality in the present Philippine context.

5. Fely Carino, *Religion and Society: Towards a Theology of Struggle* (Manila:Forum for Inter-disciplinary Endeavors and Studies, 1988) 11.

6. Carlos Abesamis, "Total Salvation, Key to Understanding the Mission of the Church in Asia Today"(Unpublished manuscript):3.

7. Mary John Mananzan, "The Religious Today and Integral Evangelization," *Lumen Vitae*, 31/3 (1976) 316-317.

8. Mary John Mananzan, "Religious Today," 321-322.

9. Statement of the Asian Women's Consulation in *Voices from the Third World*, 8/2 (December 1985): 32-33.

10. Ibid.

11. Virginia Fabella, "Mission of Women in the Church in Asia: Role and Position," in Mary John Mananzan, ed., *Essays on Women* (Manila: St. Scholastica's College, 1987), 144.

12. Mary John Mananzan, "Woman and Religion," *in Religion and Society*, 119.

13. Ibid.

14. Ruben Habito, "Spirituality:Attuning to the Breath of God," in *Asia's Gift to a Total Christian Spirituality* (Manila: Zen Center for Oriental Spirituality in the Philippines, 1988), 7.

15. Sr. Elaine MacInnes, "What is Oriental Spirituality," in *Asia's Gift to a Total Christian Spirituality*, 5.

16. Ibid.

Part Three

DOING THEOLOGY AS ASIAN WOMEN

10

Towards an Indian Feminist Theology

Aruna Gnanadason (India)

The expression "feminist theology" is usually received with suspicion and even hostility in some quarters in India. In my mind it is a very apt term for one of the most important contemporary theological movements in the church the globe over and therefore I continue to use it. What we mean by feminist theology in India, and in fact the Third World, is *theology from the perspective of women in struggle.* Because it was women's movements/struggles against oppressive structures in society that were at the root of any women's movement in the church. Feminist theology was the response of churchwomen to the systemic sin of patriarchy which lies at the root of all oppression. This new theological movement emanated not due to force of renewal within church structures, but from secular women's movements in society which had raised new questions and had formulated new paradigms in research and interpretation. Women of faith in the Church began to relook at their biblical faith based on the belief that "the Bible offers a liberating word for our times and that the feminist critical consciousness which has emerged over the last century can unlock new meaning in scripture. Contemporary feminists are asking new questions and forging new theories to enrich the religious understandings of all women and men".[1]

The Women's Movement in India

It is important to very briefly trace the history of the present phase of the women's movement in India as a foreword to an understanding of the development of a feminist theology in India. The women's movement in India can be traced to the 40s and the Telengana Peasant uprising in British India. Women in the movement organised themselves to fight against the double oppression they experienced—the economic exploitation and bondedness to the zamindars they shared with the men in their communities, which was only aggravated by the sexual violence they were particularly vulnerable to. However, when the Telengana movement was ruthlessly suppressed by the British, with it was suppressed any revolt by the women. After a brief spell of organised strength during the freedom struggle (which encouraged largely middle and upper class women to participate) women retreated into their homes till the 1970's. The incident which sparked off the present phase of the women's movement was the rape of a 14-year-old girl, Mathura, by two policemen in a lockup in Maharashtra in 1978. The Supreme Court rescinded the High Court judgement which had indicted the two policemen, on the grounds that there was not enough circumstantial evidence to prove that it was a rape. This incident created a furore among women all over India (particularly among the urban middle class) who came together and protests were launched in the major cities. Fortunately, the spurt of anger did not die down with this incident, because it was only one expression of the pent up rage of women who had for centuries borne silently the indignities heaped on them.

From here, there was no turning back, what began as an urban/middle class movement has now moved into rural India. Some evidences of this are: in 1982, a 10,000 strong procession of rural women marched through the streets of Madurai, braving the rain, and demonstrated their solidarity on the occasion of International Women's Day on March 8. They focused on issues such as unequal wages and the violence against women; in 1986, more than 5,000 rural women converged into Madras City after a 4-day-long march from Arakkonam town through hundreds of villages. They drew attention to the economic and cultural oppression of women. Women from the villages joined the march all along the way. In February, 1988 in Patna, Bihar, around 1,000 women, largely rural women, participated in a four-day national meeting where they discussed issues such as women and work, women and communalism, women and violence, women and health, and so forth. In an attempt to give the space to rural women, women from city-based organisations had opted out of participating in this now regular national gathering of women held in different parts of India. As a culmination of this meeting 10,000 women, with a few male supporters, took out a march through the city of Patna and concluded their show of strength with a public meeting which was addressed by working class women from different sectors.

What began as a forum against rape has now included a wide range of important issues among which are issues relating to dowry, to domestic violence, to unjust and archaic personal laws and other secular laws, to women and health and to the abuse of medical and genetic technology, to the media's abuse of women, to unequal and low wages, to the right of organisation and to the right to maternity and other benefits. The women's movement has gone far beyond what are traditionally called "women's issues" and has been concerned with issues such as the growing religious fundamentalism and the concurrent spate of communal violence in different parts of the country, and the indiscriminate dependence on technological solutions to what are in fact political problems of underdevelopment and poverty and the impact that this "science and technology approach" has on women. Ecological destruction and the assault on the integrity of creation have also been on the agenda of the women's movement. These are just a few of the concerns women are engaged in.

There is evidence in India, as in other parts of the globe, of various feminist theories that have formed the ideological basis of women's movements. The bulk of women's groups in India recognises the system of oppression, patriarchy, as not simply synonymous with androcentricism or sexism. It is understood as a system of graded subjugation and hierarchical relationships which specifies women's oppression in terms of class, caste, race, religion and gender. Patriarchy defines not just women as the "other" but also all subjugated peoples, races and castes as the "other"—all those who are dominated over. The interlinkage of all forms of oppression and the double or triple oppression women face within patriarchal structures are the basis of political thought of a large section of the women's movement in India. This can be explained through an analysis of the plight of a rural poor dalit woman in a village in Karnataka, who is burdened by the weight not only of her class and her caste but also of her gender. Her liberation does not lie in purely economic or political terms, her social and cultural liberation must also be taken into account. Thus the traditional Marxist analysis of oppression has proved to be inadequate and women of autonomous women's groups are now working out new paradigms of analysis from a feminist perspective. The *andro*-centric, *euro*-centric models of analysis and development that have dominated political and economic thought and which have become the universal mode have been seriously challenged.

Clearly, this new feminist paradigm takes into account the need to be in solidarity with all oppressed groups. While the focus will be on the specific forms of oppression women face and on their autonomous action, the strategy will include working with all progressive forces—be they workers' movements, peace movements, health movements, ecology movements, human rights groups, and so forth. In spite of the various feminist theories that do exist, it is to the third category that the majority of Indian women adhere, and it is that political thought that forms the basis of my thinking and is the background of these talks.

Women and Religion

"*Sati* is the only way for a woman to prove she is pure."[2]

"If any woman comes forward to commit the sacred sati at Hyderabad, the water problem will be solved immediately."[3]

The debate on women and religion has only now gained some recognition in the women's movement in India. Women in the movement have by and large, particularly Hindu women, rejected religion outright because of its patriarchal content. However there is a growing consciousness that the wholesale rejection of religion has played into the hands of conservative elements. Women are becoming aware that they need to reappropriate their religions and save them from the hands of right wing political and communal forces who would "use" the scriptures for their own purposes. This change in approach among women is evident in recent attitudes expressed in *Manushi,* the feminist magazine in India.[4]

However, it is true that religions and scriptures have been misused through the ages to legitimise fundamentalist, triumphalistic trends and have been the causes for "keeping women in their place". The present controversy raging over the debate on *sati* between Swami Agnivesh (the modern day Vivekananda) and the Shankaracharya (supreme teacher of a Hindu temple) of Puri a case in point. While we may smirk at the Shankaracharya's stance, his attitude is unfortunately not very different from that of fundamentalist and literal interpreters of the Bible. Demanding silence of women, treating women as property, denying to women their rightful place in ministry, including ordained ministry—are all biblically explained away, time and again, from the pulpits of our churches. In the face of the new activities and claims of women, many people use the Bible to protect the status quo. They engage in meticulous literal interpretations of texts to define all differences between men and women. Usually the myth that women was created second, out of Adam, is treated as evidence that she is inferior to man. In the minds of many, she is not simply different from him, she is subordinate, even evil.[5]

Churchwomen's Response

Feminist theology in India grew out of a commitment to the church and the new wind that is blowing across the land, namely, the women's movements in society. Just as there are many feminist theories that exist in the world, so "similarly, diversity in approach is also found among feminists in biblical religion and feminist theologians. There exists not one feminist theology or *the* feminist theology, but many different expressions and articulations of feminist theology."[6] It is in such a context that we must recognise the emerging Asian or more specifically Indian feminist theology as a significant articulation of the faith expression of women in this part of the globe.

But there are similarities and basic points of agreement among all feminist theologies. They all "introduce a radical shift into all forms of traditional theology, for they insist that the central commitment and accountability for feminist theologians is not to the Church as a male institution but to women in the churches, not to the tradition as such but to a feminist transformation of Christian traditions, not to the Bible as a whole but to the liberating word of God, finding expression in the biblical writings."[7]

Feminist theology is not an attempt to make some small changes in traditional theology to make it more acceptable to women. Feminist theology provides a clear paradigmatic shift in biblical interpretation. This is because the point of departure here is women's experience in their struggle for liberation.

The energy that has shaped feminist theology and the politics that has determined its hermeneutical principles are defined by the secular women's movement. It is therefore a liberation theology.

Transforming a Pyramid into a Rainbow [8]

This is how Dr. Stanley Samartha describes the challenge that lies in the way of Asian Christian women, it certainly holds true of the task before Indian Christian women in particular. Often we are criticised for imitating the West and are told that this new movement has no roots in India. In fact the Indian Church has systematically undermined the spiritual contribution and theological experience of women. Dr. Samartha writes, "Feminist hermeneutics is a subject that is hovering around the edges of Asian Christian theology but has not yet entered the centre stage. It is an attempt to look at the authority and interpretation of the Bible from the perspective of women in Asia. It should not be regarded as derived from, or imitative of, feminist movements in the West although many insights from them have influenced its temper and mood. Asian societies too are patriarchal, and the scriptures of Asian religions also legitimise male domination of women in the hierarchical power structures of society. Women of different religious beliefs and ideological convictions in Asia have been struggling against this for many years, perhaps not so vocally and aggressively as elsewhere."[9]

The other problem Indian women face is that most male liberation theologians in India have not made a serious attempt to recognise the systemic discrimination against women. Concerned as they are with the social justice dimension of theology they have been vociferous in their support of struggles for liberation of peasants, dalits, tribals and other oppressed groups, and rightfully so. These have been correctly recognised as a "spiritual necessity"[10] of our times. However, the structural violence against women, patriarchal institutions and negative attitudes to women have not been adequately analysed theologically, nor have they been recognised as "sins" against half the population of India.

James Cone in his autobiographical book *My Soul Looks Back* writes: "Why have black theologians been silent on this point (sexism) when we have been relentless in our critique of the racist practices of the white churches? I do not see how we can keep our credibility as 'liberation theologians' and remain so unliberated in our dealing with the question of sexism. Nearly all black theologians have either ignored sexism completely or have made such irrelevant comments on it that silence would have been preferable."[11] Indian women face a similar predicament. Occasional lip service is paid to the cause of women, sometimes we hear it said that there are no theological reasons against women's participation but when it comes to acting on some of the demands made by women for ministerial, theological or administrative participation, there are enough "theological" arguments given to put women down.

A recent example is what has happened in the Church of South India Madras Diocese. In March 1987 when the ordination of Deaconess Sr. Betty Paul was announced, a group of individuals filed a civil suit in the High Court of Madras challenging her ordination. With great difficulty and amidst a lot of tension the stay on her ordination was lifted an hour before the time of the services and she was ordained. However, as long as the case is in the Court, she cannot perform any of the sacramental duties of the presbyter; she will continue to assist a presbyter. The writ includes arguments that have been used to legitimise injustice against women for centuries. The usual argument used to indicate that the secondary status accorded to women is divinely ordained are that Eve was made after Adam out of his rib and she was the cause of the advent of sin and pain in the world; that Jesus had no women disciples; that Paul had called on women to be silent in the church and submit to their husbands; and that according to Levirate law, women are unclean.

But in spite of these constraints the Holy Spirit has been at work and efforts are being made by women in India to attempt a theological exploration from the socio-political economic context in which they find themselves. The rainbow will break through the dark clouds and shine! While there were some sporadic efforts earlier it was only in 1984 that an ecumenical group of women with a few men came together "to draw from the liberating influence of the gospel in an authentic effort to transcend patriarchal structure"[12] This Consultation was organised by the All India Council of Christian Women, a Unit of the National Council of Churches in India; the Association of Theologically-Trained Women in India; and a group of Catholic women. More than sixty women and men drawn from various Christian denominations, from different parts of India, reflected on the present status of women in Indian society.

We listened to the anger and deep hurt of a mother whose daughter had been murdered for dowry and to a battered wife who had escaped from her domestic prison. We discussed problems such as dowry, rape, prostitution. "Other issues that provided anger and resentment were related to women in the church and the marginalised role accorded even to those who were 'ordained'. To the churches a call was made to refuse to solemnize marriages where dowry is given or taken. Also to strike down outdated laws through the introduction of a uniform civil code, particularly in the context of marriage, divorce, adoption and succession. The churches were further exhorted to give a theological reinterpretation to human sexuality, and to revitalise theological education in seminaries and in sermons so as to bring about a sensitivity to the humanhood of women in an attempt to strengthen the community of men and women at the ecclesial level."[13]

In all this however, we sought a theological dimension, an explanation, a challenge to discover "not only a new way of looking at things, a new subjectivity, but an interpretation of historical processes from the perspective of the losers. In this way we recapture the dimension of resurrection for past sufferings and defects and open up a new path into the future."[14]

With this being the beginning, several other efforts at encouraging women to do a "historical critical re-reading of biblical and extra-biblical traditions in order to retrace the struggle of our fore-sisters for full humanhood and to re-appropriate their victories and their defects as our own submerged history"[15] have been made by the organisations and women involved in the first exercise. Other organisations have done their share.

The Challenge before Women

One thing is clear: there *is* the need for new paradigms of theological search for women. While it is true that Indian women have not worked out a clearly defined *Indian feminist hermeneutic*, their contribution to theological development must be recognised. A group of Indian women after a discussion on a Biblical Reflection on the National Situation wrote.

"It is difficult in the Indian context to directly theologise as we must be conscious that Christians in this country are just near three per cent of the total population. Therefore any theologising must be done with an awareness of India's multireligious background and of the need to build a common culture and participate in secular political processes. The secularness of the Indian polity must be safeguarded at all costs by *all* citizens and institutions including the churches, and we must be cautious to avoid communalism and communal misunderstandings in our theological endeavours.

"However, we as a group of women felt that our concern for the sacredness of human life, justice and freedom finds strong support in the roots of our faith and therefore we need to rethink our traditional theological heritage which has largely remained indifferent to the distortions of our social system and political life and has attempted to confine our interest to personal piety and salvation of individual souls. At the same time the churches have often made indirect or even outspoken arrangements with the powers that be. Quite in contrast to this heritage we see God as one who comes to vindicate the oppressed. God is continuously intervening in history, including Indian history, so as to judge those who grind the face of the poor, those who deprive the widow and the orphan. It becomes essential for Christians to theologise because God's intervention not only judges the injustice of the present social order but comes to create a new one. We must be alert to discern how we can participate as co-creators with God in the establishment of a new society."[16]

It is basically this concern to find meaning for the suffering of all people and particularly of women, that any attempt is made to re-read and reinterpret the Bible from the perspective of women in India. For Indian Christian women the need is to transform the liberating word of God from a boring book which has submerged women into silence and submission, into a challenge that will bring new life and energy to them to participate with God in co-creating a new and living community.

There are still people who would claim that there is only one theology and there could be no feminist theology. Such a stand is in itself to be severely criticised because it is based on an assumption that there is a possibility of having a value-free neutral theology (which is ironically largely Western and androcentric) in the church which is placed in a crisis- ridden world. But I hold that separatism by women or any other marginalised group is only a strategy and only temporary so as to prepare the whole community for a new world of human relationships. And anyway, "to advocate the women's liberation movement in biblical religion as the hermeneutical center of a feminist critical theology of liberation and to speak of the church of women does not mean to advocate a separatist strategy but to underline the visibility of women in biblical religion and to safeguard our freedom from spiritual male control."[17]

This is our main concern, that the question of women is *not* merely a demand for more positions in decision making or more power in church administration; it is that but it is more than that. It is a plea to recognise women's theological and spiritual contributions as an integral part of the churches' prophetic ministry in the world. It was interesting to read how Tissa Balasuriya of Sri Lanka calls for a "new hermeneutic" to connect feminism and the liberation of theology itself. Quoting from Balasuriya, Dr. Samartha writes: "The Scriptures themselves are to be subject to a transforming influence. They are not total revelation of God to humanity: they are only one such revelation. We cannot limit God and God's message to the whole of humanity to only a few from a male-dominated society. We cannot limit God to one generation or impose silence on God after the death of the last apostle."[18]

What Then Can Women Do With The Bible?

It is clear that the Bible cannot be spontaneously reappropriated by women, i.e. we cannot just read the Bible through the eyes of women, because we cannot deny the fact that the Bible is an androcentric text written by men in a patriarchal context. The peasants of Solentiname were able to spontaneously reappropriate the text to understand the oppression and exploitation of the masses of Nicaragua; however, we as women cannot do this.[19] The Bible which is often factually interpreted to keep women "in their place" cannot be separated from its patriarchal content. For example, the prophets of Israel protest against the hierarchical, urban, landowning society that deprives and oppresses the rural peasantry. God is here seen as a critic of this society, a champion of social victims. However, gender discrimination is not questioned. Rosemary Radford Ruether writes, "Although Yahwism dissents against class hierarchy, it issues no similar protest against gender discrimination... there is always a sociology of knowledge in social ideology even in liberation ideology. Those male prophets who were aware of oppression by rich urbanites or dominating empires were not similarly conscious of their own oppression of dependents—women and slaves — in the patriarchal family."[20]

Indian women will not easily *reject the Bible* because of its patriarchal content. We are growing in consciousness that we cannot afford to do so. We have to reclaim biblical religion as our own heritage because "our heritage is our power".[21]

There is another way open to women and that is a *reclaiming of the Bible as a feminist resource* because, in spite of its misuse, it has also through history, provided authorization and legitimization for struggles for human dignity and justice— there is clearly a liberation strand. The Bible inspires us to re-read it with a commitment to women's liberation in particular and human liberation in general. Mary Ann Tolbert points out that feminist biblical scholarship is profoundly paradoxical because "one must struggle against God as enemy assisted by God as helper, or one must defeat the Bible as patriarchal authority by using the Bible as liberator."[22] Women of the church have inherited a history of early Christianity which has "been written from the perspective of the historical winners"[23] and has sanctioned the continued control of all power, including theological power, in the hands of dominant groups in the present day church. What women will try to continuously do is to draw strength from their biblical roots, so as to open up a path into the future. This yearning for a new future, a new community, cannot be minimised because it is a song for freedom from the dust into which women's humanity has been crushed for centuries.

Our task as Indian women is clear—to search for a feminist hermeneutic which will carry all women and the whole church towards becoming a new and living community in Christ.

NOTES

1. Barbara Brown Zikmund, "Feminist Consciousness in Historical Perspective," in *Feminist Interpretation of the Bible,* ed. Letty M. Russell (Philadelphia: The Westminster Press, 1985), 29.

2. Niranjan Dev Teerth, Shankaracharya of Puri in *The Stateman,* quoted in *India Today,* 15 May 1988.

3. Niranjan Dev Teerth, Shankaracharya of Puri in *The Sunday Observer,* quoted in *India Today,* 15 June 1988.

4. *Manushi* is a feminist magazine of some repute that is published in Delhi by a collective of women. It provides not only investigative articles on women in India but also a theoretical analysis and background to understanding the questions women are raising.

5. Barbara Brown Zikmund, "Feminist Consciousness," 22.

6. Elisabeth Schussler Fiorenza, *Bread Not Stone: The Challenge of Feminist Biblical Interpretation* (Boston: Beacon Press, 1984), 3.

7. Ibid.

8. S.J. Samartha, *Search for New Hermeneutics in Asian Christian Theology* (Bangalore: Board of Theological Education of the Senate of Serampore College, 1987), 34.

9. Ibid., 33.

10. K.C. Abraham, "A New Spirituality" in *Break Every Yoke: Abraham Malpan Memorial Lectures* (Ecumenical Christian Centre Publication, 1983), 60.

11. James H. Cone, *My Soul Looks Back* (Maryknoll, New York: Orbis Books, 1986), 121-122.

12. Stella Faria, "A Reflection on the National Consultation: Ecumenicity of Women's Theological Reflections," in *Towards a Theology of Humanhood: Women's Perspectives*, ed. Aruna Gnanadason (ISPCK, Delhi: All India Council of Christian Women(AICCW), 1986), 2. This National Consultation was organised by AICCW with the Association of Theologically-Trained Women and Catholic Women as a first stage of the Ecumenical Association of Third World Theologian's (EATWOT) programme of the Working Commission of Theology from the Women's Perspectives.

13. Ibid., 3.

14. Gabrielle Dietrich, "The Origins of the Bible Revisited: Reconstructing Women's History," in *Towards a Theology of Humanhood*, ed. Aruna Gnanadason, 34.

15. Ibid., 33.

16. "The National Situation: A Biblical Response from Women," *Stree Reflect Series* 1 (1986). This series is published by the AICCW.

17. Elisabeth Schussler Fiorenza, *Bread Not Stone*, 7.

18. Tissa Balasuriya, "Feminists and the Liberation of Theology" in God, Woman and the Bible, *Logos* 22/31 (October 1985): 94; quoted in S.J. Samartha, *Search for New Hermeneutics*, 41.

19. Ernesto Cardenal, ed., *The Gospel of Solentiname* (Maryknoll, New York: Orbis Books, 1987); quoted in Gabrielle Dietrich, "Perspectives of a Feminist Theology: Towards the Full Humanhood of Women and Men," *Woman's Image Making and Shaping*, ed. Peter Fernando and Frances Yasas (Ishvani Kendra Pune, 1985), 123.

20. Rosemary Radford Ruether, *Sexism and God-Talk: Towards a Feminist Theology* (London: SCM Press Ltd., 1983), 62-63.

21. Elisabeth Schussler Fiorenza, *Bread Not Stone*, xiii.

22. Mary Ann Tolbert, "Defining the Problems" in *The Bible and Feminist Hermeneutics* (Scholars Press, 1983), 120; quoted in Letty M. Russell, ed., *Feminist Interpretation of the Bible,* 140.

23. Elisabeth Schussler Fiorenza, *In Memory of Her: A Feminist Theological Reconstruction of Christian Origins* (New York: Crossroad, 1983), 83.

11

Feminist Theology in the Korean Church

Ahn Sang Nim (Korea)

It was during the latter part of the 70s that feminist theology entered the picture in Korea and became an issue among some women in the Korean Church. The term is still not too familiar, and some are still uncomfortable about it because it sounds like the shouting of some high-powered women. Some say, "What kind of theology is that? If there is feminist theology, there should be masculine theology, too." But feminist theology came into being precisely because theology has always been nothing but male dominated, and the Bible has always been interpreted only by men. Men have dominated theology and the Church to the exclusion of women. In the formation of theology, women, half the world, have been excluded in the reflection and voice of human experience.

Twenty years after I graduated from the theological seminary, I found the real meaning of the gospel through feminist theology, and now I am studying theology again. Today, I would like to share what I have learned through feminist theology.

It seems to me that feminist theology has resulted from the education of women, together with a change in theological trends. After women were educated, those trained theologically came to realize that theology and biblical interpretation have always been expressed by men's voices, reflecting only male experience. It has been said recently by theologians that the Word of God is understood differently according to the situation of the reader. We cannot expect the same reaction from everyone. What is understood by or what impresses one may be perceived differently by another. Even reading the same Bible verses, I get a different impression this year than when I read them last year. Also I get a different understanding or meaning depending on whether I am happy or sad when I read them. How, then, can one expect a man, whose experience is totally different, to represent women's understanding of the Bible.

So, feminist theology is raising questions about issues that until now theology and Church tradition have presented only from a male viewpoint, to the exclusion of women's voice or experience. Theology developed only by men without the participation of women, who make up half the world, can only be half a theology. We need to produce a whole theology by adding the other half—theology from the viewpoint of women.

Feminist theology is concerned about God and God's concerns. God created the world and in God's image God created men and women and made them stewards over the world. God is concerned that those who turn away from God return to God, recover the relation between God and human beings and recover the broken relationship among human beings as equals, as God created them. This broken world would be healed and restored to the world God created. Then all the different people would be able to live together in harmony, living at peace with God and one another in this beautiful world.

Feminist theology strives toward such a world of harmony and peace; that is why feminist theology is called a theology of harmony and a theology of peace. Feminist theology believes in the coming of such a kingdom of harmony and peace. Today's sexism is not the order God wants. In the light of the coming kingdom, we realize that sexism is wrong and try to change it into an equal relationship. Accordingly, feminist theology is a way of responding to those people who believe that God is calling us for that purpose. It is a journey of people who are determined to break down the rock of patriarchy, who are trying to remove the rock while singing together and crying together. Feminist theology is not a struggle simply to be women but to be human beings. So it is not a struggle for women to be above men, but for women and men to be equal. It will not be a lonely way for us. It is a journey of faith during which we believe the Holy Spirit will be with us all the way. The Holy Spirit, which was promised by Jesus, will encourage us and help us until the rock has been completely removed.

WOMEN'S PERCEPTION OF GOD

To begin the journey, let us think, first of all, about theology being done by women. Theology is talking about God. It is talking together about what we think about God as holy, almighty, fearful, everlasting, Father, King of kings, Lord of lords, judge, warrior, etc. Most of these images of God are patriarchal. God has been perceived as a powerful male, a father with absolute power. Such a theology confessing such a patriarchal God has established a patriarchal hierarchy in a patriarchal church. In such a church, women have lost their position of equality with men and have become devalued, marginalized.

In John 1:18 we read, "No one has ever seen God." Human beings cannot see God, so everyone describes God by a different image. The image of God should be drawn from every sphere of human experience. The experience of men and women, rich and poor, workers and employers, educated and non-educated, young and old, healthy and ill or disabled, should all be included in describing the image of God. Yet in Christianity God has been described mostly as father.

When women became able to read the Bible, they found different images of God. After Eve and Adam ate the forbidden fruit they first wrapped themselves in fig leaves, and "the Lord God made for Adam and his wife garments of skins, and clothed them" (Gen 3:21) From this, women see God sewing garments like a mother sewing clothes for her children.

In Isaiah 46:3ff, it is written: "Hearken to me, O house of Jacob, all the remnant of the house of Israel, who have been borne by me from your birth, carried from the womb... to gray hairs I will carry you... I have made, and I will bear; I will carry and will save." A woman having had the experience of birth pangs can say, "Ah! God is like a mother."

The prophet Hosea describes God in the second chapter as follows: "The more I called the more they went from me... Yet it was I who taught Ephraim to walk, I took them up in my arms; but they did not know that I healed them. I led them with the bands of love, and I became to them as one who eases the yoke on their jaws, I bent down to them and fed them." Here, a woman sees a mother raising her children with loving and tender care. She can think of God as a mother's lap where she can cuddle up with a cozy feeling. If God is like such a mother, I should not be trembling or fearful, or afraid of God. I can be free to talk to God about my life, my needs, with an easy mind. It is a great feeling not to be afraid of God; so great that I feel as though I could fly. This could never happen when God's image was that of a strict father, a fearful judge. Then I came to understand why God came to earth, to human beings, telling them how much God loves them. If my children were away, I would come to find them, and ask them to believe I love them and just want them to come back home. It seems to me that the Roman Catholic Church solves this human need through devotion to Mary. Human needs cannot be met with only a father image of God. There needs to be a mother as well, and this is found in Mary, the mother of Jesus.

THE BIBLE AS READ BY WOMEN

By reading the Gospels through women's eyes, let us see how Jesus rejected the patriarchal system and set women free.

Jesus was conceived by the Holy Spirit, was born of the virgin, Mary, who had never "known man." When Korean women were campaigning for amendment of the Family Law, they faced strong opposition from Confucians, who would even risk their necks to retain the Family Law because of the importance of the male seed or sperm. It seems to me that by being conceived of the Holy Spirit, without this power of a man's sperm, Jesus rejected the patriarchal culture. When I began to think about it I became very excited. Just think! Jesus came into this world only through a woman. No man did anything to bring Jesus into the world. I learned later that this idea had already been written a few decades ago by Karl Barth in his Church Dogmatics, in the article "The Miracle of Christmas." Born of the Virgin

Mary means being born not because of male generation but solely because of female conception." (Church Dogmatics 1/2 p. 185) Jesus came to this world rejecting a man's genealogy, one to be proud of, as in Matthew where his genealogy is traced back to Abraham. Jesus came solely through the body of a woman.

Jesus' purpose for coming is found in Luke 4:18-19: "To preach good news to the poor, to proclaim release to the captives and recovering of sight to the blind, to set at liberty those who are oppressed, to proclaim the acceptable year of the Lord." Women are the poor. Men have vested interests but women do not. Women are oppressed under the patriarchal culture. Women are captives of sexism. Women cannot see out from behind men. To such women Jesus came to preach good news. Jesus came to proclaim the acceptable year of the Lord, the year of Jubilee. In Leviticus 25 we read, "You shall hallow the fiftieth year and proclaim liberty throughout the land to al! its inhabitants. It shall be a jubilee for you." It was God's command to return property to its original owner and to set the slaves free. In the Old Testament, however, there is no record of a jubilee being celebrated. Because human beings could not follow God's will, finally Jesus came into the world in a human body and proclaimed that these things were happening here and now. "Today this scripture has been fulfilled in your hearing" (Lk 4:21).

Now let us hear how Jesus freed women. You remember how Jesus healed a woman who had had a flow of blood for twelve years. At that time women's bleeding was considered an uncleanness. In Leviticus 12 we read of the rite of purification of the uncleanness of a mother after childbirth. "If a woman bears a male child, then she shall be unclean for seven days. Then she shall continue for thirty-three days in the blood of her purifying; she shall not touch any hallowed thing, nor come into the sanctuary until the days of her purifying are completed. But if she bears a female child, then she shall be unclean two weeks and she shall continue in the blood of her purifying for sixty-six days." Here again, we see how the rule of sexism applies to a woman from birth.

In Leviticus 15 there are regulations about women's discharge and the rite required to take away her impurity. "When a woman has a discharge of blood which is her regular discharge from her body, she shall be in her impurity for seven days, and whoever touches her shall be unclean until the evening. And everything she lies or sits on shall be unclean... If she is cleaned of her discharged, she shall count for herself seven days, and after that she shall be clean. And on the eighth day she shall take two pigeons for burnt offering and sin offering." When women were bound by such severe laws for their regular bleeding, how could a woman who had been bleeding for twelve years expect even decent treatment as a human being? She could neither go out of her house nor touch anybody. Yet such a woman dared to touch Jesus' clothes. At that time, no man would speak to a woman, even his wife, in public. So, according to Jewish law, this woman had commited a great sin. Yet Jesus called her out in front of people and announced that she had been cleansed by her faith. He rejected the patriarchal law and set her free as a whole person.

Let us look at another case. You will remember the woman who was so impressed by Jesus' teaching that she shouted,"Blessed is the womb that bore you, and the breast that you sucked!" (Lk 11:27). This was praise to the mother who had given birth to a great person. This woman was shouting while she was imagining how happy Jesus' mother would be. It was not at all a strange expression, because it was a culture in which women were thought to be instruments for childbirth. In Genesis 16, Abraham's wife, Sarah, was so worried at not being able to have a son that she sent her maid slave into Abraham's bed to assure the succession of his name. Jacob's wives did the same thing. In Ruth 4, Ruth bore a son to Boaz, who was next of kin to her husband, to succeed her husband. (cf Deut 25:5) These cases show us how important is the succession of a man's name in Jewish law and how women were used for that purpose. In a society with such a law the woman's praise mentioned above was a very natural expression. Even nowadays we praise the mother when we talk about a great person. But Jesus said,"But blessed rather are those who hear the word of God and keep it." This was rejecting the image of women as childbirth machines. He rejected the custom by which a woman's body was used as an instrument of succession for a man's family name.

Feminist theology follows such teachings of Jesus. Today in our society a woman's body suffers from sex torture, sexual violation, sex tourism, heavy labour and commercial advertisements. This is not what God wants for human beings. A woman's body should not be seen as a luxury sex object, nor should it be sacrificed for industrial growth. One of the aims of feminist theology is that women be seen and respected as human beings created in the image of God. In this way men also recover their rightful image as human beings.

THE DISCIPLESHIP OF WOMEN

We will now deal with women's discipleship. One of the reasons most Korean Churches do not ordain women is that Jesus and his disciples were all men. Let us learn about the women who followed Jesus. The woman who met Jesus at Jacob's well was the first missionary to witness to Jesus as the Messiah. Martha of Bethany confessed Jesus as the Christ, just as Peter did. With the same confession, the man, Peter, became the founder of the Church, but not much of the story of the woman, Martha, is left to us. Recently scholars have said that there had been a book of the Acts of Martha, just as there was one of the Acts of the Disciples. We can say Martha was Jesus' disciple just as Peter was.

Luke 8 shows us a picture of women disciples. "And the twelve were with him and also some women who had provided for them out of their means." Those women were taking the role elders take in the Korean Church today. When Jesus was carrying the cross the male disciples, who ate and stayed with Jesus, all ran away. On the other hand, on the way to Golgotha there were weeping women who had followed Jesus all the way from Galilee. Jesus told them, "Do not cry for me, cry for yourselves and your children." It seems to me Jesus told them to take care of the next generation.

After Jesus was buried in the tomb, the male disciples hid themselves, but the women went to the tomb to care for Jesus' body. Since he was crucified on the cross, a death only for political criminals, his tomb was heavily guarded by soldiers. Nobody would dare to come to his tomb. Yet early in the morning Mary Magdalene and other women went to Jesus' tomb to anoint his body. The risen Jesus sent these women to his hiding disciples to witness to his resurrection. Even though women could not speak in public at that time, Jesus sent women as his witnesses to his male disciples. Later on these women received the Holy Spirit along with the men at Mark's upper room. Yet, we are told it is against the Bible to ordain women.

When the early Church began, women offering places for worship and for people to gather together played a central role in the establishment of the body of Christ. Women spoke in tongues and offered public prayer in the Corinthian church (1Cor 11). But when the expectation of Jesus' imminent second coming was delayed beyond the end of the first century, men returned to the old order of patriarchalism. Let us read some verses which show that attitude. "The head of a woman is her husband...any woman who prays or prophesies with her head unveiled dishonours her head: let her wear a veil "(1Cor 11:3:5). "As in all churches of the saints, the women should keep silence in the churches. For they are not permitted to speak, but should be subordinate, as even the law says. If there is anything they desire to know, let them ask their husband at home, for it is shameful for a woman to speak in church" (1Cor 14:34-35). "I urge that supplications, prayers, intercessions, and thanksgivings be made for all men... I desire that in every place the men should pray...Let a woman learn in silence with all submissiveness. I permit no woman to teach or to have authority over men: she is to keep silence" (1Tim 2). These verses have been good excuses to exclude women from the clergy for the past two thousand years. That is why Paul is blamed for sexism. But Paul declares in his first letter to Galatians. "For as many of you as were baptized into Christ have put on Christ. There is neither Jew nor Greek, there is neither slave nor free, there is neither male or female; for you are all one in Christ Jesus" (3:27-28). Those who have been baptized are free of any discrimination of sex, race, or class. Baptism is a sacrament, a call to equal discipleship. We who are baptized and have confessed Christ are all disciples of Jesus Christ. Among Christians there should be no discrimination. Therefore, refusing the ordination of women or their exclusion from decision-making bodies, while leaving to them all the burden of kitchen work in the church today, is an influence of patriarchal culture. Jesus set women free two thousand years ago!

Paul also worked with women. In Romans 16 Paul greets his fellow workers. Ten out of the 28 persons listed are women. "Our sister Phoebe, a deaconess of the church at Cenchrae, that you may receive her in the Lord as befits the saints. She has been a helper of myself. Prisca, my fellow worker in Christ, Mary who has worked hard among you, Junias, my fellow prisoner, workers in the Lord, Tryphaena and Tryphosa, the beloved Persia, who has worked hard in the Lord, Rufus 'mother, Julia and Nereus' sister.'' These names have been noted through the study of feminist theologians. Realizing that Paul had written these names, I believe Paul practiced what he had declared in Galatians of the dismantling of sexism.

Feminist theology opens our eyes to read the Bible with new understanding. I would like to quote from Elisabeth Fiorenza's model of biblical interpretation. "Feminist critical interpretation begins with a hermeneutics of suspicion. It takes as its starting point the assumption that the biblical text and its interpretations are androcentric and serve patriarchal functions. It develops a hermeneutics of proclamation. It must be complemented by a careful theological evaluation of biblical texts and their oppressive or liberative impact in specific culture situations. It develops a hermeneutics of remembrance that moves from biblical texts about women to the reconstruction of women's history. Finally, it moves from a hermeneutics of disinterested distance to a hermeneutics of creative actualization that involves the church of women in the imaginative articulation of women's biblical story and its ongoing history and community."

Feminist theology cannot be completed only by studying with the head, but it should also be accompanied by living out the theology in practice. Feminist theology in the Korean church must begin from the experience of the oppression of women. We have to analyze the reason for their oppression and get rid of the cause, remove the rock. It is our task to remove the rock of sexism from the Korean Church. That is one way to mend this broken world in accordance with God's will.

OUR TASKS FOR THE NEXT TEN YEARS

First of all, let us begin with the study of the Bible. I would ask all of you who are participating in this gathering to form small groups of five or six persons around you. Reading the Bible together from a feminist theological perspective, we will be able to hear the Word of God today. Exchanging experience with each other, sharing our pain, encouraging each other and helping each other, we will grow as persons who live knowing the gospel rightly. Then we will become agents of mission, spreading God's Word to others with great joy, understanding what real good news is. Then we will be able to remove the patriarchal rock from our church.

Second, the church is the body of Christ, so men and women should participate equally in all its activities, committees and gatherings. We have to change our attitudes, customs and systems to enable men and women to work together in decision-making and in activities of services. As a result, many women elders and ministers should be ordained and they should be able to find places to serve without difficulty, and they should receive equal treatment with men in similar conditions.

Third, it is discrimination against women and the trampling of women's humanity which allow women to be subjected to sex torture, sex tourism and commercial advertisement. Low wages or no wages for women's work is treating women as if they were not authentic human beings. We must fight against sexism in our society by uniting with women, both religious and secular. In order to remove the basic rock of legal discrimination, all Korean women should work in solidarity for such things as the amendment of the Family Law.

Fourth, our beautiful land where we were born and where we will be buried, is being destroyed by industrial development and is dying from pollution. God is calling us to participate in the restoration of this broken world. We must repent of our lifestyle, which has been directed toward consumerism, luxury, and competition for the top. Instead, we must turn to the reformation of life, the protection of nature, use less of its limited resources, and share our resources with others to preserve them for future generations.

Fifth, remembering the oppression of women because of their sex, we must remove the rocks of discrimination among human beings so that all people who suffer discrimination in this society and the world might be respected as human beings created in the image of God.

Sixth, we must eliminate sexist and discrimination factors from all the church's educational material. We must make the task of the humanization of women and men in the whole educational process a first priority.

Finally, Korean people have suffered deeply from long years of national division. Now, North and South should repent our hatred of each other. Women from the North and South should meet together and laugh together so we can start the great work of national reconciliation. Our people will be revived after we have removed the rock of national division. The way for our people to be revived is by removing the rock of poverty, disease, and suffering from the powerless who have been exploited and oppressed by the powerful of this world. This is exactly what God will accomplish when God's Reign is finally established in this world.

Feminist theology is the way for all Korean Church women to take up these tasks together, and the way for all women and men in the world to hold hands and band together. This is the road to removing thousand of years of the old patriarchal culture with the help of the Holy Spirit which was promised by Jesus Christ. Today, God is calling us, "Christian women of Korea! Let us remove this rock together."

Dear sisters and brothers, let us together start to remove the rock of patriarchal culture which is in front of us in the Korean Church and in the whole world.

12

"Han-pu-ri": Doing Theology from Korean Women's Perspective

Chung Hyun Kyung (Korea)

I

Last April in New York I had the chance to see an exhibition of recent woodcut prints from the Korean people's movement. When I entered the exhibition room I was overwhelmed by the power of the work. I cried. I cried because I could see the opening of a new horizon in these prints, something I had been longing for in my theological work for a long time: discovering, naming, claiming, and creating our own reality. I could not see any apologetic attitude in these prints. They simply said what they felt, with confidence. They trusted their experience.

A Korean art critic who had brought the prints talked about the cultural movement of young artists in Korea. Most were well trained, he said, in the Western fine-arts style. However, they had overcome the cultural captivity of Western art and had created their own styles which could express the content of people's everyday lives and their struggle for liberation. The artists' personal styles mirrored the style of our national heritage.

This same concern was demonstrated several years ago in Korea in a landmark exhibition of paintings entitled "Vomiting," where, for example, a painting done in the Western high-art style was covered with Korean cartoons. From the time of this exhibition, the most vital of Korean artists have sought to evolve an art which could give a life-giving power to the Korean people. One artist whose works were included in this exhibition emphasized the key to this change in people's art; it was the artists' belief in their own aesthetic feelings as opposed to a need for approval from their teachers or Western standards.

I call these artists and myself second-generation liberationists. Our teachers, who were the first-generation liberationists, mainly reacted against the colonial heritage. They did not realize that they were involved in a subconscious attempt to prove themselves to their former colonizers. They said they knew their enemies and could think as well as or better than their colonizers. Our teachers clearly knew what they did not like but they did not know where they should go in their own works. We members of the second generation owe a lot to our teachers because they gave us the colonizers' tools and the space to create. We second-generation liberationists are not unaware of the neo-colonial power surrounding us but we also know our own power. We know what we like and we construct our own life-giving works. We believe in our experiences and are not intimidated by outside authorities any more.

Doing theology from a Third World woman's perspective must be understood in this context. My teachers' generation felt compelled to prove their theological abilities (in descending order) to white male theologians, white feminist theologians, and finally Korean male theologians, in order to justify the validity of Korean women's theology. But in my generation we start our theology from owning our own feelings and experiences. We know that the most dangerous thing for an oppressed people is to become benumbed through internalizing alien criteria and ignoring our own gut feelings. If we do not permit ourselves to fully experience who we are, we will not have the power to fight back and create our own space. We have to touch something really real among and around us in order to meet God. Just as young Korean artists from the people's movement find their aesthetics in ordinary people's everyday lives, so we emerging women theologians find God's revelations in our ordinary everyday experiences. As the artists use Korean styles to express their artistic aspirations, so too we theologians try to use our national and cultural traditions to express the God-experiences of our people.

I do not try to articulate Korean women's God-experience from biblical or orthodox theological perspectives in a traditional sense. Instead I like to name Korean women's experience within our cultural context of suffering and life-giving using our traditional symbols and metaphors in an organic way. Then I try to make connections between Korean women's experiences and the Christian tradition. In this article I will approach Korean women's God-experiences through our overwhelming sense of the presence of haunting ghosts in our land.

II

I was raised in a ghost land. My childhood memories are filled with various kinds of haunting ghosts. Ghosts are everywhere. There are kitchen ghosts, toilet ghosts, house ghosts, river ghosts, and mountain ghosts.

As a young girl, it was difficult for me to live with so many ghosts. I knew ghosts would hurt me if I did not behave. I heard awful stories about ghosts from many people. They said most ghosts carried swords in order to kill people whom they hated. These ghosts were the spirits who could not rest because what had happened to them in their earthly lives was too cruel and unjust to forget or forgive. They were therefore wandering around seeking the chance to inflict revenge or to tell the truth.

Even though I could not see them, I always felt the ghosts' presence. I was afraid of them. I was especially afraid of baby and children ghosts. I should be careful not to make them jealous of me. Too many cookies, too many toys, or too many beautiful clothes might make baby and children ghosts angry at me. I had to share with other children. Otherwise baby or children ghosts would not tolerate me because they had never had the privilege to enjoy those things in their short earthly lives.

I never went outside by myself after sunset. Whenever I wanted to go to the bathroom, which was located outside the house in Korea, I went there with an adult. I kept the bathroom door open while I was doing my business because I was afraid of bathroom ghosts. People said bathroom ghosts had bleeding hands which pulled people into the dung hole. I also never slept by myself. I always slept with adults until I was thirteen.

There were some fun moments in the ghost land. One of them was watching the ancestor worship. The ancestor worship was a really big family event. Many relatives gathered together, prepared meals and had big feasts. We opened all of the windows and doors to let our ancestors into the house. Ancestors were friendly ghosts. Most of them had families to take care of their tombs and to remember them. They were not wandering ghosts. They rested in paradise and visited us annually on the ancestor worship day.

Ancestor worship day was like home coming day for all of us. At midnight we lit candles and burned incense and worshipped them. All the men in the household bowed down to the ancestors' spirits. My mother, aunts and I watched the worship from outside the room when my father, uncles, and brother bowed down. I was very envious of my brother. As a little girl I could not understand why I was not allowed to bow down to my grandfather's and grandmother's spirits. I loved them too! One ancestor worship day—I think I was five or six years old — I cried and screamed, asking my father to let me join the ancestor worship. I kept crying, lying on the ancestor worship room floor. Finally my father let me join him.

In Korea women prepared the feasts but they were not allowed to participate in the worship itself. I felt sorry for my mother. However, she was in charge of feeding all of the visitors, including the wandering ghosts. She always left generous amounts of food in front of the main gate of our house for wandering ghosts. She said to me she should not forget to leave food for the wandering ghosts as they did not have relatives to take care of them. Mother told me they were constantly hungry. My favourite part of the ancestor worship was the feast. We shared food after finishing the ancestor worship and shared our life stories with one another until dawn.

Another fun activity in the ghost land was watching in my neighbourhood the shamanistic rituals we call "Kut." Since my mother was a Christian, she did not want me to see Kut. Therefore I had to go there without my mother's knowledge. There was always music, dancing, and excitement in Kut. I felt my body was moving, following the drum beat. The shaman wore beautiful, colourful dresses and sang and danced until she reached a state of ecstasy. She then called to the ghosts and talked to them. Other times the shaman consoled the ghosts, played with them, or negotiated with them. There were many people who watched the shaman and responded to her.

During my junior and senior high school days I gave up my interest in ghosts. The Korean public education system, which was influenced by the pragmatism of John Dewey, brainwashed me into believing that all ghosts stories were superstitious fantasies. It was an age of enlightenment and independence. I could sleep alone and go to the bathroom courageously by myself!

The ghost world returned to me when I went to college and studied Korean history with others in the student movement. It was a revelation for me. I realized Korean history was full of wars, invasions, and the cruel exploitation of my people by foreign powers and domestic power elites. So many people have died unjustly throughout our history. Where have all these people gone? Where are they now: heaven or hell? According to Korean beliefs, these people's spirits could not rest in eternal peace. All of these people had to become restless wandering ghosts!

Since my college days wandering ghosts have not been objects of fear for me. I started to believe that these ghosts were the voices in the wilderness which could unveil and proclaim all of the unjustices in our history. I must listen to their voices because they must clearly contain God's voice as it has resonated throughout our history.

In Korea we call these wandering ghosts Han-ridden ghosts. "Han" is a very peculiar feeling. According to the late "Minjung"[1] theologian, Suh Nam-Dong, Han is "the suppressed, amassed and condensed experience of oppression caused by mischief or misfortune so that it forms a kind of 'lump' in one's spirit."[2] This is the typical, prevailing feeling of the Korean people. Another Korean Minjung theologian, Hyun Young-Hak, described our deep, shared feeling of Han very vividly:"Han is a sense of unresolved resentment against injustice suffered, a sense of helplessness because of the overwhelming odds against us, a feeling of total abandonment ('Why hast thou forsaken me?'), a feeling of acute pain of sorrow in one's guts and bowels making the whole body writhe and wiggle, and an obstinate urge to take 'revenge' and to right the wrong all these constitute."[3]

This feeling of Han comes from the sinful interconnections of classism, racism, sexism, colonialism, neo-colonialism, and cultural imperialism which Korean people experience everyday. I want to think of Han as the Korean people's "root experiences" or "collective consciousness." I think any meaningful Korean theology must start from the understanding and articulation of Han. Korean Minjung theology arose out of this consciousness in the 1970s.[4]

The direct translation of "Minjung" is "people." But Minjung is not a neutral term. Minjung means a specific people. According to a Korean Minjung theologian, Suh Kwang-Sun, Minjung are "the oppressed, exploited, dominated, discriminated against, alienated and suppressed politically, economically, socially, culturally, and intellectually, like women, ethnic groups, the poor, workers and farmers, including intellectuals themselves."[5] Therefore the term "Minjung" is a bigger and broader concept than the "proletariat." Minjung theologians try to articulate theology out of the concrete historical experience of the Korean Minjung.

Korean women's theology shares many things with Korean Minjung theology. However it clarifies the content of oppression further. Just as Mercy Amba Oduyoye named the Third World women's status as "irruption within the irruption,"[6] we Korean women could name our status as "minjung within the minjung."[7] Korean women have taken within their whole being the poisons of injustice and suffering in our history and have survived. She was at the bottom of the oppressive system but has not always been a passive victim. The Korean woman is also an agent of liberation. She has given birth to a new life and hope for our country.

III

What are the specific aspects of Korean women's Han? In order to articulate Korean women's theology out of Korean women's root experience, Han, we have to know the concrete context of Korean women's Han. Korean women have been suffering with Korean men under colonialism, neocolonialism, and military dictatorship throughout our painful history. The oppression of women, however, has taken specific forms in addition to all of the experiences of suffering that women share with men. I want to call this aspect of women's suffering "gender specificity." Women suffer just because they are women. The people with power of domination have exploited women in particular ways using the female gender ideology. I would like to unveil the Korean women's Han in the perspective of the gender specificity of women's suffering. While I am uncovering the mutilated "her-story" in Korean history, I will also try to discover the signs of active resistance within women's culture. Sometimes Korean women were destroyed as "passive victims" due to lack of power bases and support systems. Other times Korean women were "active agents" of liberation and wholeness for both men and women in our society. Following are some prototypes of women's suffering or active resistance in Korean history.

Women's Han under religio-cultural gender ideology

In ancient Korea, Korean women enjoyed more or less equal status with men. We can find the traces of matriarchal society in Korean history. However, since the time Korean society was organized into rigid social and religious systems, female gender has been the target of oppression and exploitation. Especially after the Yi dynasty which established Confucian ethics, women's oppression has deepened. (Confucianism was based on the adult male leadership in the family and others' obedience in the name of harmony.) The elite group of the Yi dynasty developed the ideology of female chastity and obedience.

Once women's sexuality and chastity belonged to her family, women had to live under severe sexual censorship because, under the Confucian social order, losing her virginity hurt the social advancement of male members of her family. For example, they prevented widows from remarriage. Widows' remarriage, it was thought, made the blood of the family unclean. Women are responsible for the purity of their family's blood. When a widow got married, she was punished along with her parents, new husband, and children by blocked social advancement of the whole family. Even a ten-year old girl who was engaged through her parents' arrangement had to keep to her widowhood in the in-laws' house if her future husband died before marriage.[8] The young never-married widow's life was constantly guarded by both families. In some cases a young widow's room was locked and she was prohibited from coming out — in order to maintain her chastity. The young girl's sexual desire was the object of her family's fear. In the worst cases, the young widow was encouraged to commit suicide or she was secretly killed to keep the family reputation intact. Even now we see the presence of this oppressive culture when unmarried women living singly is discouraged or when widows are encouraged to maintain their celibacy. Korean women have endured all such social, cultural, and religious control over their lives. But they have also actively fought against double standards in our cultural and religious life by creating and sharing songs, poems and stories among women.[9]

Women's Han under colonialism

Under Japanese colonization many Korean women's bodily integrity was violated by Japanese colonial and military power. During World War II, Japan recruited poor, rural Korean women for their labour forces. These women were forced to be official prostitutes for Japanese soldiers. About one hundred thousand Korean women were used by Japanese soldiers in the various battle fronts. According to one Korean woman who survived the war, she and others had to receive Japanese men all through the day and night.[10] Even though their private parts were swollen and they cried from pain, the women were forced to continue to receive the soldiers.[11] Many Korean women died of venereal diseases. Other Korean women were either abandoned in foreign lands or were killed by the soldiers when the Japanese retreated from their battle lines. When Japanese soldiers reported the death toll to their superiors, they simply reported these women's deaths as "a few lost war supplies."[12] Some Korean women survived this hell. Many of them could not return to Korea, however, because they were ashamed of themselves and "virtuous" Korean morality would not accept these "dirty" women back. Many of them died in alien lands. The Japanese government deliberately destroyed the reports on these Korean women. Their pain could thus be erased permanently from history. I am sure these women have become wandering Han-ridden ghosts.

Women's Han under neo-colonialism

The struggle of women workers at the Tongil Textile Company shows the sinful interconnection between neo-colonialism, military government, and sexism. Tongil Textile Company was an export-oriented company. As in many other textile factories, the majority of workers were women. Behind the rapidly increasing GNP of Korea in the 1970s there were many women workers who worked under miserable conditions in the textile companies. These companies provided the main materials for Korean export. At Tongil Textile Company about 80 percent of the workers were women. Male workers originally led the union. Women workers' consciousness was raised by their participation in the labour movement and they finally elected a woman as their union leader.

Some of the male workers who belonged to the union would not tolerate a woman as head of the union so they received money from the company and tried to destory the woman-led union with the help of the police. Women workers were disillusioned by this betrayal by their male comrades and resisted. When this resistance became stronger some of the male workers and policemen threw faeces and urine at the women. Some women workers were force-fed on faeces and had their breasts smeared with faeces. All this did not destroy their struggle. Rather, it made the woman-led union stronger. When police tried to arrest them by force, women workers took off their clothes and protested naked. This symbolic action made a qualitative leap in the Korean women workers' movement. Rev. Cho Wha Soon, who staunchly supported the women workers, confessed that this event raised her and other women's consciousness as women.[13] Before the event, women workers did not pay much attention to the women's movement because they considered it a middle-class movement. But after the betrayal by their male comrades, they began to realize their need for liberation from sexism. When the women workers of Tongil Textile Company took off their clothes they also took off male domination over their lives.

Women's Han under military dictatorship

Kwon In-Sook, a twenty-three year old labour activist who was expelled from her university for her involvement in the student movement, was arrested in June 1986 as a subversive. Police detective Moon Kwi-dong (thirty-three years old) began examining her on alleged connections with other people in the movement. When she refused to reveal the names, the police detective took off her clothes, beat her and sexually tortured her.[14]

Ms Kwon was deeply humiliated. She confessed that she wanted to kill herself due to extreme shame and pain. Her liberationist consciousness would not allow her to commit suicide. She decided to let the whole world know what she experienced. She wrote out a request to arrest the torturer, her request was discarded by the chief of security. Upon hearing of the incident, women prisoners who were in the same prison as Ms Kwon went on a hunger strike in order to support her. The next day the male prisoners did the same.

This was the first time in Korean history that a woman made a public issue of sexual violation. Many Korean women have been sexually tortured in various circumstances by the officers of the dictatorial government but they did not dare to speak out for fear of endangering their families' reputation and out of fear of revenge by the government. Ms Kwon broke the culture of silence on violations of women's sexual and personal integrity which were prevalent in Korea under the military government.

Children's Han under poverty

Women's Han is not just limited to adults. Children accumulate Han in their hearts too. Children are deprived of their childhood in the poor sections of Korean society. Let us listen to the poem written by a twelve-year old Korean girl in a slum:

My mother's name is worry,
In summer, my mother worries about water,
In winter, she worries about coal briquets,
And all the year long, she worries about rice.

In daytime, my mother worries about living,
At night, she worries for children
And all day long, she worries and worries.

Then, my mother's name is worry,
My father's name is drunken frenzy,
And mine is tear and sigh.[15]

When poverty is the order, the people who suffer most from poverty are women and children. A Korean woman organizer, Kang Myung-soon, lives in a slum area and has talked about children's Han in her community. Once some five-or six-year-old children in her community went to a wealthy church and were taunted as dirty beggars by some affluent children whose families belonged to the church. These children asked Kang Myung-soon to return with them to attack the wealthy church. The children carried stones in their hands.[16] When these poor children grow up and their individual Han join to become a collective Han, what kind of future can Korean society expect?

IV

How can we then solve and untangle the accumulated Han of Korean women? In Korea we call the release of Han "Han-pu-ri." I think Han-pu-ri must be the purpose of doing women's theology in Korea.

Originally the term "Han-pu-ri" came from Korean shamanistic tradition. Korean shamans have played the role of the priest/ess of Han-pu-ri in his or her communities. Shamanistic Kut (ritual) gave the opportunity for the voiceless ghosts to speak out their stories of Han. The community then must solve the Han of the ghost collectively either by eliminating the source of oppression for the ghosts or by comforting or negotiating with the ghosts. Therefore Han-pu-ri has been an opportunity for collective repentance, group therapy and collective healing for the ghosts and their communities in Korean society.

The most fascinating things about Korean Han-pu-ri for me are the following three factors.

1. The majority (65-70 percent) of Shamans who play the role of the priest/ess of Han-pu-ri Korean society are women.
2. The majority of people who participate in the Han-pu-ri Kut in Korean society are women.
3. The majority of characters in ghost stories are women.

These factors provide an important clue for the "hermeneutics of suspicion." But why are women the majority in the above situations? When I look at the three factors with the "epistemological privilege" of the Third World women, the answer is clear. Korean women have been the embodiment of the worst Han in our history. They usually did not have the public channels to expresss their Han. This developed a sense of impassibility among Korean women. Many of them died without releasing the sense of impassibility in their lives. That is why there are so many women ghosts in our traditional stories. Women who endured the helpless impassibility could understand one another through their shared life experience as women. Han-pu-ri became one of the few spaces where poor Korean women played their spiritual role without being dominated by male-centred religious authorities. Han-ridden women got together and tried to release their accumulated Han through Han-pu-ri Kut.

There are three important steps in Han-pu-ri. The first step is *speaking and hearing*. The shaman gives the Han-ridden persons or ghosts the chance to break their silence. The shaman enables the persons or ghosts to let their Han out publicly. The shaman makes the community hear the Han-ridden stories. The second step is *naming*. The shaman enables the Han-ridden persons or ghosts (or their communities) to name the source of their oppression. The third step is *changing* the unjust situation by action so that Han-ridden persons or ghosts can have peace.

The Korean Association of Women Theologians (KAWT) developed a theological methodology by which they can assuage Korean women's pain. KAWT follows steps which are similar to the shamanist Han-pu-ri when they articulate Korean women's theology.[17] According to the report of their second consultation for the establishment of feminist theology in Asia,[18] women theologians took the following steps. They started their theologizing from listening to the Han-ridden women's stories. They invited women from the bottom stratum of Korean society such as farmers, factory workers, and slum-dwellers, and listened to their life stories. After this step, the women theologians did social analysis with the help of social scientists and other women who knew the structural aspects of the problem. They then moved to the theological reflections with the questions raised by the former two steps. The next step was to check with the original storytellers and communities whether the articulated theology made sense to them and empowered them. The final step was action. KAWT participated in various demonstrations and organized protests in order to solve Korean women's Han.

I can find four main theological sources in the Korean women's emerging theologies. The most important source for Korean women's theology is the Korean women's lived experience. However, this experience is not the universal, abstract,and standardized human experience as alluded to by some traditional European male theologians. The specific historical experience of Korean women is manifested in their experience as victims and agents of liberation, and through the experience of Han and Han-pu-ri. Korean women's experience is the starting point and ending point of Korean women's hermeneutical circle. The second source is critical consciousness. Critical consciousness is different from a neutral, detached, objective reason. Critical consciousness is an engaged subjective reason which takes sides. Critical consciousness is the thinking power which can uncover the ideology of domination. The third source is tradition. Korean women use all of the traditions we have in order to fully articulate Korean women's theology.

We use our own religious traditions such as Shamanism, Buddhism, Confucianism, and Christianity, and political ideologies. However we do not use all the traditions uncritically. We distinguish from a specifically women's perspective the liberative traditions from the oppressive traditions. We women learn from our experiences that male-defined liberation did not always include women's liberation. We use liberative traditions to empower women and use our critical analysis of the oppressive traditions to name the source of oppression. The fourth source is scripture. We use the Old and New Testaments along with other scriptures from our traditional religions. We selectively choose liberating messages from the texts. Scriptural texts are our references for women. We learn by the texts, but we go beyond the texts to meet the community behind the text.

When we Korean women do theology with the above methodology and resources, we come up with the question of the norm for our theology. What makes our theology good theology? I will say the norm of Korean women's theology is the power of liberation (Han-pui-ri) and life-giving. If a theology untangles the Korean women's Han and liberates us from bondage, it is a good theology. If a theology keeps us accumulating our Han and staying in our Han-ridden women's places, it is a bad theology no matter how important church unity, the authority of the Bible, and church traditions are. If a theology has a life-giving power to Korean women and empowers us to grow in our full humanhood, that is a good theology. If a theology makes us die inside and wither away in our everyday bodily and spiritual life, it is a bad theology.

Can this Korean women's theology be a Christian theology with these two norms: liberation (Han-pu-ri) and life-giving power? Surely it can because we Korean women believe in *good* news (gospel), not bad news. For us, the gospel of Jesus means liberation (Han-pu-ri) and life-giving power. In that sense, we are Christians. Where there is genuine experience of liberation (Han-pu-ri) and life-giving power, we meet our God, Christ, and the power of the Spirit. That is good news. We Korean Christian women define our Christian identity according to our lived inherited experience which stretches five thousand years back, even beyond the birth of Jesus.

NOTES

1. "Minjung" is a Korean word meaning people, specifically, oppressed people. Korean theologians did not translate Minjung theology as people's theology in order to emphasize the particularity of Korean people's historical, cultural experience.

2. "Towards a Theology of Han." *Minjung Theology,* Singapore, CCA, 1981, p.65.

3. "Minjung the Suffering Servant and Hope," a lecture given at James Memorial Chapel, Union Theological Seminary, New York, 13 April 1982, p.7.

4. Suh Kwang-sun's article, "A Biological Sketch of an Asian Theological Consultation," in *Minjung Theology* (pp. 15-37) shows the origin and the development of Minjung theology in the Korean context.

5. From Suh Kwang-sun's class lecture given at the School of Theology at Claremont, August 1983.

6. "Reflections from a Third World Woman's Perspective: Women's Experience and Liberation Theologies," in *Irruption of the Third World,* New York, Orbis, 1983, p. 247.

7. Letty Russell used the similar term "Minjung of the Minjung" in order to name the Korean women's status. See her forthcoming article "Minjung Theology in Women's Perspective," to appear in a book of critical reflections on the development of Minjung theology in Korea (ed. Lee Jung-young, to be published by Orbis).

8. For the resource for women's life under Confucianism, see Lee Ock-kyung, "A Study on Formational Condition and Settlement Mechanism of Jeong Juel (Faithfulness to Husband by Wife) Ideology of Yi Dynasty," an MA thesis, from Ewha Women's University, Korea, 1985.

9. For concrete examples, see Lee Oo-jung, "Korean Traditional Culture and Feminist Theology." *The Task of Korean Feminist Theology*, Seoul, Korean Association of Women Theologians, 1983, pp.63-78.

10. *Prostitution: Study on Women*, No. 2, Seoul, Korean EYC, 1984, p.13.

11. *Ibid.*

12. *Ibid.*, p.14.

13. Personal interview with Rev. Cho Wha-soon, New York, May 1986.

14. This fact sheet is based on a report of the Korean National Council of Churches Human Rights Association, printed in local edition of *Dong-A il bo*, New York,

17 July 1986.

15. Taken from the cover page of *My Mother's Name is Worry: a Preliminary Report of the Study on Poor Women in Korea,* Seoul, Christian Institute for the Study of Justice and Development, 1983.

16. Kang Myung-soon, "The Story of Poor People," in *Korean Culture and Christian Ethics*, Seoul, Moon Hak Kwa Chi sung sa, 1986, p.381.

17. This is not the official position of the Korean Association of Women Theologians, but my personal interpretation of KAWT's theological methodology.

18. Korean Association of Women Theologians, *Second Consultation for the Establishment of Feminist Theology in Asia*, Seoul, KAWT, 1983.

13

Final Statement:
Asian Church Women Speak

(Manila, Philippines, Nov. 21-30, 1985)

INTRODUCTION

We, church women from Hong Kong, India, Japan, Korea, Malaysia, the Philippines, and Sri Lanka, bound by a common vision of a just and free society, have come together from November 21 to 30, 1985, in Manila, Philippines, to reflect theologically on Total Liberation from Asian Women's Perspective.

We belong to different Christian denominations; we come from diverse and complex cultures and backgrounds, but we experience a common bond and a common bondage—as Asians and as women.

In this light, we came together to reflect on the situations we find ourselves in and to examine the effects of these realities on the lives of our people particularly the women.

During our first days in the Philippines, we exchanged views with Filipino women from different sectors of society. We also immersed ourselves, even for only a very short while, among the poor and oppressed—the farmers, the workers, the fisherfolk, and the urban poor—and experienced for ourselves the deplorable conditions they are in.

During the consultation, we shared experiences and insights, we discussed and analyzed, at times with much pain and effort, in order to understand one another and the realities that surround us. We later realized, however, that we did not delve deeply enough into other important facets of our Asian roots—the great Asian religions and traditions that have shaped our Asianness.

We examined the contributions we have made and the role we have played in the past, even as we planned for the tasks we have to undertake in the future. In silence and prayer, with dances and songs, we celebrated and offered to God our hopes and joys, our wounds and pains—as Asians and as women.

REALITIES AND ANALYSIS

We are alarmed by the increasing poverty and oppression engulfing Asia today, resulting not only in the dehumanizing of persons but also in the extreme degradation of women. Foreign domination, state repression, militarization, and racial strife have reduced our people to being mere pawns in the deadly games of the powerful. In the interplay of these evil forces, it is the women who suffer most.

In all spheres of Asian society, women are dominated, dehumanized, and dewomanized; they are discriminated against, exploited, harassed, sexually used, abused, and viewed as inferior beings who must always subordinate themselves to the so-called male supremacy. In the home, church, law, education, and media, women have been treated with bias and condescension. In Asia and all over the world, the myth of the subservient, servile Asian woman is blatantly peddled to reinforce the dominant male stereotype image.

Indian women still live under the shadow of a patriarchal tradition that manifests itself in violence against women, namely, the dowry system, bride burning, forced sterilization, and sex-determination tests. Hindu mythology, which depicts woman as the seductress or the evil one incapable of moral self-control, has helped to institutionalize these unjust practices.

Filipinos, like many of their Asian sisters, are subjected to job discrimination and are exposed to health hazards in factories, multinational corporations, and export processing zones. Because of the severe economics crisis, and with the advent of sex tourism and the presence of U.S. bases, many Filipino women and children have been plunged into prostitution. Many leave home to become migrant workers in hostile alien lands. Furthermore, many are raped, tortured, imprisoned, and killed for their political beliefs.

In Malaysia, where there is a resurgence of religious fundamentalist trends, widening economic inequalities, worsening communal relations, and diminishing political freedom, women are the worst hit. In Japan, the male-oriented emperor system is still firmly established. And even as the people continue to bear the stigma of the nuclear havoc wreaked upon them, Japan steadily moves into a highly dangerous technological stage with its concomitant deadly hazards.

In Korea, people suffer from pain of separation and division of their homeland; they live under a government preoccupied with national security and militarism, while remaining in the grip of the Confucian family law that makes men absolute masters in all aspects of life.

Oppression of women cuts across class, caste, creed, race, profession, and age. But even among women there is division and misunderstanding because of differences in perceptions.

Living in the Third World, we see and experience double oppression from the all-pervading patriarchal system deeply ingrained in our societies, aggravated by the unjust structures which have been perpetuated by the rich and the powerful in collusion with the foreign forces that dominate us.

In the midst of all this political, economic, and cultural turmoil, strong people's movements are emerging, with the women contributing great force and militance to these movements. Women's growing awareness indeed heralds new life and liberation from the shackles that have long stifled us. We have reason to rejoice and be hopeful.

THEOLOGICAL REFLECTIONS

In our theologizing, we attempted a creative and collective work style, which we felt mirrored the vision of that community toward which we are striving. Instead of working individually on separate papers, we developed composite papers on six theological themes in relation to women. In the process we uncovered hidden realities and arrived at conclusions:

Oppression of women is SINFUL. This systemic sin is rooted in organized and established political, economic and cultural structures with PATRIARCHY as an overarching and all-pervading reality that oppresses women.

As church people, we have come to realize that the highly patriarchal churches have definitely contributed to the subjugation and marginalization of women. Thus we see an urgent need to reexamine our church structures, traditions, and practices in order to remedy injustices and to correct misinterpretation and distortions that have crippled us.

We saw how theology itself has added to these distortions. We unearthed theological premises, traditions, and beliefs that have prevented us from becoming fully human and have blurred the image of God that we are. These elements are:

—the patriarchal image we have of God;
—the predominant male interpretation of the Bible;
—the overemphasis on the maleness of Jesus, which has been used to discriminate against women in the church and society;
—the propagation of a ''Mary cult,'' which not only vitiated the person of Mary, but also dislocated her and minimized her active role in salvation history; and
—the bias against woman in Christian tradition buttressed by male-oriented Asian religious beliefs.

On the other hand, we rediscovered Christ's liberating and salvific mission which encompasses all; we encountered the Christ of the poor; we saw his power over sinful structures and situations. Most of all, we felt confirmed by Christ's radical breakthroughs and supportive stance for women during his time.

We saw Mary, the mother of Jesus, no longer as a passive, ethereal being, detached from the suffering millions of Asia. We now see her in a new light, as a strong woman who can identify and be with today's grieving mothers, wives, daughters in the bitter fight for freedom.

Even as we identified repressive elements in other religious traditions, we recognize that there are also life-giving elements in these great Asian traditions.

In the process we recognized the need for new symbols and an inclusive language to formulate a theology that is contextual and liberating, as well as a need for renewal in the churches and in communities of faith so that *koinonia* will be realized.

Through all our reflections, we were aware of the Holy Spirit's bonding presence among us. Thus we prayed to the Holy Spirit—that our varied gifts and insights may be welded into one powerful tide to help overcome the forces of death and evil, and usher in the New Creation in Asia.

TOWARD COMMITMENT AND ACTION

We, Asian church women, declare our strong solidarity with our oppressed people—the workers, the farmers, the fisherfolk, the urban poor, the tribal and ethnic minorities, and most especially the women—in the painful struggle for full humanity.

We denounce foreign domination, state repression, militarism, dehumanizing capitalism, and all forms of evil that subjugate women.

We offer our collective strength and power to our Asian sisters in the fight against poverty and oppression.

We staunchly support women's movements in confronting patriarchal structures and traditions; we are one in struggling for democratization in the home, the church, the schools, and society in general.

We will constantly exercise vigilance in upholding women's right to equality and self-determination; we will work unceasingly to lift our suffering sisters—the battered, the tortured, the hungry, the silenced, and the unfree.

We firmly resolve to promote authentic feminist education and the development of a liberating theology from the perspective of Asian women.

We strongly encourage new forms and ways of communication that will make us aware of issues that affect our lives and our fortunes.

We reach out and join hands with our sisters beyond our shores. Together we will rise from our bondage and heal wounds; together we will continue to hold up half the sky and move mountains.

WE CALL FOR UNITY AND SOLIDARITY, FOR IT IS ONLY BY WORKING TOGETHER TOWARD A NEW COMMUNITY OF WOMEN AND MEN THAT THE WORLD WILL WITNESS THE COMING OF THE NEW KINGDOM, WHICH IS THE EMBODIMENT OF JUSTICE, EQUALITY, PEACE, AND LOVE.

14

Conference Statement:
Consultation on Asian Women's Theology

(Singapore, Nov. 20-29, 1987)

We, 32 delegates from 16 countries in Asia,met in Singapore, November 20-29,1987 and reflected prayerfully on theology in the light of our national and regional situations, especially the situation of women.

The Situation of Women in the Region

Many governments of the region claim to be democratic but are not authentically so. There is large scale misuse of power at various levels, affecting the lives of the majority. Extremes of poverty and wealth, corruption, wide-spread unemployment, and oppression of minorities exist alongside one another. In many countries this has provoked organised revolt and confrontation from different sections of society. In some situations the government has assumed an increasingly repressive and authoritarian character by their use of law and courts or by their expansion of police and paramilitary apparatus. There is a culture of militarism alongside classism, racism and castism.

The international operations of western capitalism intrude into our countries, as does the arms race and the threat of nuclear war.

All of these situations are the outcome of institutionalised patriarchy, and they underlie even the apparently most democratic nations.

Within this general situation, it is the women who suffer the most because of their sex and the restrictions culture places on women. They are oppressed in the church as well as in society. Often sexism is sanctioned by religion.

The exact form of sexism varies from country to country but within each culture women are marginalised in a number of ways. Sexism erupts into overt violence, e.g. in rape, domestic violence, sexual harassment, incest, prostitution, pornography, female foetucide, infanticide and sati. Customs like dowry can also lead to violence. Even in countries where discrimination against women is outlawed, customary attitudes to women mean that, as in other countries, women are less well educated than men in general, are given jobs of lower status, and receive lower income than men. Women often work in bad conditions. They often live in poverty. Higher education often does not lead to good jobs or higher income, and can lead to more demanding work and social expectations. The education of women is wasted instead of being used for development of society and church. Within both church and society, women are excluded from decision-making bodies, even when the matters they are considering affect women's lives directly.

Few churches actively encourage women to study theology. Women hold up the church and are most of the congregations, but the number of women in decision-making bodies and in theological colleges does not reflect the number of women in the church. Very few churches ordain women and the number of ordained women is still very small. Ordination of women has not led to structural change which is liberating to women. Until now, the church's theology has been done by men, and women's experience and spirituality has had no place in their work. The same is true of indigenous people who suffer colonisation and invasion.

Emerging Asian Women's Spirituality

Asian women identify and define spirituality as faith experiences which motivate our thought processes and behaviour patterns in relation to God and neighbour. Spirituality is awakened souls urging dignified humanhood.

Traditional spirituality was understood to be individualistic and inward looking. It is passive and distinguishes holy from the non-holy. In contrast, contemporary spirituality is integral, out-going, community-oriented, active, holistic, and all-embracing.

The challenges of the new spirituality are manifested in our dying to ourselves in order to live for others. Feminist spirituality is prophetic and has a mission with commitment. It is born of a new vision. It challenges the technical, scientific and capitalistic world. The new spirituality involves a change in this world so that Jesus Christ is incarnated in our lives enabling us to discover our own identity and strength. This strength enables women to struggle for their well-being and survival, for human rights, social justice and peace; to participate in socio-political, economic, culture life and decision-making processes; to struggle against the caste system and for equality of tribal and all oppressed people and structures. Feminist spirituality empowers us against sexism.

The Holy Spirit

The trinitarian image of God gives us a great insight into the whole process of creation of the world with human beings made in God's image. The spirit is understood as the all-pervading presence and the moving force of

God. The Holy Spirit in relation to women is a life-giving, comforting, liberating and creative Spirit. It is a powerful Spirit who empowers women as individuals and also as community.

The Holy Spirit enables us to have a unitive vision of reality. From an inherited, male dominant theology, we move to a theology of partnership in Asia, which in the true sense can be called as Asian Human Theology.

Women's Understanding of Christ

The Asian women's understanding of Jesus is that of one who transcends the evil order of patriarchy. Jesus is the prophetic Messiah, whose role is that of the suffering servant, who offers himself as a ransom for many. Through his suffering Messiahship, he creates a new humanity. In contrast is the classical view of God as male and of the Christ as the male image of God. In this traditional view, Jesus is a triumphal king and an authoritarian High Priest. This view has served to support a patriarchal religious consciousness in the church and theology. It has justified male dominance and perpetuated the subordinate status of women. The evil patriarchal order which subjugates and oppresses women in society is seen to operate also in the church. But women participate in the messianic prophetic role of Jesus through the suffering of oppressed women and through the solidarity and struggle of women who seek freedom from patriarchal structures.

Who is Mary?

It is the task of all women to reclaim Mary and redefine her as liberator of oppressed people, especially women of all ages and cultures. We reject the distortion of Mary's identity which comes from male interpretation. We claim the right to liberate the church's teaching about Mary. The doctrine of the Virgin Birth has been used to oppress women. We understand that the real meaning of the Virgin Birth is the end of the patriarchal order. We reject this order in ourselves, our families, and church and society.

The Magnificat is a rallying point for women and for all denominations to work together with the poor and oppressed to overcome injustice. We believe in a new creation in which we all claim our full humanness. We must therefore overcome economic and political oppression in our own contexts as well as in First/Third World relationship.

In response to Mary, we commit ourselves to the work of creating new partnerships.

The Church

The church and its institutions have been heretical in discriminating against women, in being hierarchical in structure and in not using the gifts which the Holy Spirit gives to all the members of the church. We challenge the church to show in its life that it believes the Gospel — that women as well as men are created in the image of God, that women as well as men are saved and set free by Jesus the Christ, and that because women and men are baptised into one Lord Jesus Christ, distinctions between men and women disappear and should not affect the life of the church. God calls the church to share in the struggle for liberation of all people, especially women. The church can only do so when it ceases to oppress its own members, and let those of its members who suffer oppression in society direct its mission.

As Asian women our theological image of the church is a circle of God's people in which Jesus the Christ is the centre. There are various inequalities in Asian society, based on sex, class, race, and the north-south divide. But in this circle, all the people are the same distance from Jesus Christ, guaranteeing full equality and human dignity. Jesus Christ being the alpha and the omega, this community, this ecclesia, this circle, aims for the final completion which is the Christian hope.

Contributors

Ahn Sang Nim, Ex-General Secretary of Korean Association of Women Theologians. Her article is the text of a speech given at the occasion of commencement of Church Women's Decade in Seoul, Korea 1988, in response to the call of the Women's Committee of World Council of Churches.

Chung Hyun Kyung, from Korea, is a doctoral candidate in systematic theology at Union Theological Seminary in New York. Her essay was original-ly published in *Ecumenical Review.*

Elizabeth Dominguez, a member of the United Church of Christ in the Philip-pines, is professor of Old Testament at Union Theological Seminary in Dasmarinas, Cavite.

Virginia Fabella, a Maryknoll Sister from the Philippines, is academic dean of Sister Formation Institute in Quezon City and the Asian Coor-dinator of the Ecumenical Association of Third World Theologians (EATWOT).

Aruna Gnanadason, a member of the Church of South India, is executive secretary of the All India Council of Christian Women and Vice-Moderator of the World Council of Churches sub-unit on Women in Church and Society.

Crescy John, a member of the Roman Catholic secular institute Khristsevikas, is research associate at Streevani Women's Research Project and ac-tive in the Women's Institute for New Awakening (WINA) in India.

Kwok Pui-lan teaches Religion and Society in the Chinese University of Hong Kong. A doctoral candidate at Harvard Divinity School, she is doing research on feminist theology in China.

Lee Oo Chung, President of the Association of Korean Women's Organisa-tion. A human rights activist and a New Testament scholar.

Mary John Mananzan, a Missionary Benedictine Sister from the Philippines, has a Ph.D. in philosophy and is dean of St. Scholastica's College in Manila.

Monica Melanchton, a member of Church of South India, presently a doctoral candidate in Old Testament at Lutheran Theological Seminary in Chicago.

Sun Ai Lee Park, from Korea, an ordained minister of the Disciples of Christ, is editor of In God's Image, an Asian women's theological journal, and is Asian Coordinator of the EATWOT Women's Commission, and Coordinator of Asian Women's Resource Centre for Culture and Theology.

Christine Tse, from Hong Kong, obtained a diploma in social work in Italy, and is Peace and Justice coordinator for the Centre for the Progress of Peoples, Hong Kong.

Lily Kuo Wang, an ordained minister of the Presbyterian Church in Taiwan, also a faculty member of the Presbyterian Bible College in Hsinchu, Taiwan.

Yong Ting Jin, a member of the Basel Christian Church of Malaysia, is the Asian-Pacific regional secretary of the World Student Christian Federation, based in Hong Kong.